Recognizing Faculty Contribution

A system for planning, organizing, documenting and rewarding faculty activity

by
Richard F. Bortz
Southern Illinois University

Training Systems Designers

Carbondale

Library of Congress Catalog Card Number
86-50266

ISBN 0-9619851-0-0

First Printing - 1986
Second Printing - 1987

Contributing Author:

Dr. M. Frances Keen
University of Miami

Cover Design
Janet Musgrave Kent

Printed in the United States of America

To Mom and Elaine,
for their interest, encouragement
and love

Acknowledgements

Several people have made significant contributions to the completion of this handbook. First, I want to thank Dr. Francis Keen for sharing her vitae with me. Fran's experience in nursing and nursing education has resulted, hopefully, in examples that are relevant and appealing to members of both the academic disciplines and professional schools.

Ms. Carolyn Lawson deserves a special thank you for her many and varied contributions. Her ability to listen, understand and add perspective to various problems encountered in writing the manuscript were invaluable. Also, when the manuscript was in its final stages of preparation, Carolyn's patience and cheerfulness in making my all-too-numerous "last changes" were very much appreciated.

Special recognition is also due Ms. Lyn Corder. Lyn's editorial experience and writing abilities added substantially to the organization and presentation of the textual material. Her awareness and knowledge of "things academic" made Lyn an excellent resource on technical aspects of the handbook.

Lastly, I want to thank Ms. Jeanne Fisher and Ms. Joni Whistle for typing (and retyping) the original manuscript. Their typing and word processing abilities, in the end, made this work a reality.

Table of Contents

Foreword

This handbook provides faculty members, chairpersons, deans and other academic officers in institutions of higher education with a plan for developing and implementing a system for recognizing faculty contribution. The book suggests a performance-based approach tailored to meet the professional growth and development needs of the faculty and, at the same time, insure the progress of the department.

The two-fold purpose of the faculty recognition system is to assist faculty members in planning, organizing and documenting their professional activities and to establish a basis for recognizing and rewarding faculty accomplishment.

The goals of the system are to:

- Assist faculty members in attaining their professional and career goals;
- Assist academic departments in attaining their organizational goals and continue providing leadership and service to their clientele;
- Foster cooperation in the department by using a system that benefits individual faculty members and the department alike;
- Establish a system for documenting and reporting faculty activities;
- Articulate salary increase, merit pay, tenure and promotion in recognizing faculty accomplishment; and
- Provide a fair and equitable means of evaluating the activities and contributions of faculty members.

The handbook rationalizes the process of recognizing faculty contribution and accomplishment. It articulates the steps of the process into an understandable and systematic whole and encourages the recognition of teaching competence, scholarly effort, service contribution and professional practice activity* as the only acceptable criteria for recognizing and rewarding faculty performance. As with any proposal that suggests change, the faculty recognition system may have to be tailored somewhat to meet the needs of individual departments and faculty members. Its adoption will not require

---

* A fourth category of activity, "Professional Practice Activities" is introduced here and appears in the examples throughout the handbook. The inclusion of this activity is to accommodate departments which encourage their faculty members to maintain a professional practice while fulfilling their academic responsibilities.

drastic changes in most situations in that it uses the accepted trilogy of teaching, research and service, plus professional practice, as its basis for planning and organizing department and faculty activity.

The handbook is organized into four parts: Department and Faculty Planning, Faculty Recordkeeping, Reporting Faculty Accomplishments, and Evaluation and Implementation. Chapters One through Nine discuss the development of the components of the faculty recognition system. Each chapter includes the rationale, organization and criteria for preparing the respective components. Sample documents conclude the chapters in the planning and reporting parts of the handbook. Chapter Ten reviews the purpose and goals of the faculty recognition system and summarizes the major concepts fundamental to its development.

This handbook was written to assist faculty members and department chairpersons in planning, organizing and documenting department and faculty activity. I hope that it helps those who read it attain these ends and, in turn, receive recognition appropriate to their effort and contribution.

Richard F. Bortz

Introduction

The central truth is that the individual's fullest use of his best talents is prompted under conditions which he has helped to determine and which he cherishes because he finds them helpful to his most satisfying self-expression and growth.[1]

An organization is a group of people that exists for the purpose of assisting the whole of society, or some segment thereof, in meeting its needs. Fundamental to an organization's success is its ability to plan, organize and manage its activities and resources. Early in the formation of an organization, the members must define their common purpose. They must establish challenging but realistic goals, align available capital and human resources, and put a system of evaluation in place to measure their effectiveness of operation.

The most important aspect of organizational management is the direction and influencing of people in the day-to-day operation of the organization. Personnel management, the art and science of dealing with employees, is predicated on the development of a set of management values that regard people as essential to the success of the organization. Implicit to this concept is management's adherence to these values in making decisions which effect the employees and recognize their many contributions.

The same general concepts employed in the management of people in a business setting also hold true for the administration of people in an educational environment. Like a business, the educational enterprise requires planning and organization to succeed. In light of the needs of its clientele, the educational institution must define its purpose, goals and mission. The institution must align capital and human resources to deliver its programs and services and measure the effectiveness of its efforts once they have been put into practice. Also, the educational institution must have an evaluation scheme in place that justly measures the performance of faculty delivering the programs and recognizes their effort and contribution.

---

[1] *The Art of Administration,* (p. 59) by Ordway Tead, 1951, New York: McGraw-Hill. Adapted with permission of publisher.

1

2

Institutional Planning

In institutions of higher education, policies that affect the recognition of faculty contribution through salary increment, merit pay, and the awarding of tenure and promotion come from the central administration. The policies are usually comprehensive in scope and generally address excellence in teaching, research, service and professional practice.

Once formulated by the chief administrators of the institution, the general policies are forwarded to the colleges for consideration. The policies are reviewed by the dean (or other designated administrator) and members of the faculty. They are either accepted as presented or refined to more precisely define excellence as it relates to faculty performance within the college.

The college then distributes the institutional and college versions of the policies to its departments. The department chairperson and faculty members review the policies and accept them as presented or refine them again to meet department standards. When finally accepted, the policies become the criteria for recognizing and rewarding faculty performance within the department.

The process that moves the faculty recognition policies from general to specific is necessary and desirable. General policy statements are appealing because of their flexibility of interpretation, but prove to be a liability if used to evaluate specific types of activity. Generally stated criteria are subjective and leave the evaluator with no definitive way of determining acceptable performance. When this situation exists, the evaluation process becomes vulnerable to personalities and politics as the criteria for evaluation.

Roles and Responsibilities

The chairperson and faculty members work together to implement the faculty recognition system in the department. The chairperson initiates development of the system and works with the faculty members in preparing departmental and individual plans, implementing them and evaluating the attainment of individual and department goals. In situations where no formal system exists, the chairperson and faculty members have the responsibility to develop a plan. If a system is already in place, but discussions reveal only partial satisfaction with it, steps are taken to identify the areas of concern and rectify them. Once a consensus is reached that a new system would help the faculty plan, organize and evaluate its activities, the chairperson then assumes a leadership role in developing and incorporating the faculty recognition system into the department's plan of operation.

Faculty members play a dual role in developing a faculty recognition system. As a group, they work with the chairperson in determining the purpose, goals and mission of the department and identifying the needs of the clientele they serve. Individually, faculty members also have a responsibility in implementing the faculty recognition system. With the assistance of the chairperson, faculty members plan their activities to meet the needs of the department and, at the same time, ensure attainment of their own career goals.

When selecting activities, care must be taken to define an acceptable balance of teaching, research, service and professional practice for each faculty member. Balance promotes departmental involvement in each of the four areas of activity. When coupled with productivity, it establishes the basis for recognizing and rewarding faculty performance.

Process

The process for developing the faculty recognition system is divided into three major steps. See Figure 1.1.

 I. Department and Faculty Planning
   A. Developing a Department Plan
   B. Developing an Annual Plan of Activities.
   C. Preparing a Semester Assignment

 II. Faculty Recordkeeping
   A. Developing an Activities Card File
   B. Developing a Samples File

 III. Reporting Faculty Accomplishments
   A. Writing an Annual Achievement Report
   B. Preparing a Curriculum Vitae
   C. Preparing a Promotion Dossier

Figure 1.1 - Process for Developing
a Faculty Recognition System

Department and faculty planning includes the development of a planning document for the department; a document for planning the annual activities of individual faculty members; and an assignment sheet for planning and assigning the semester activities of the faculty members. In the department plan, the purpose, goals and mission of the department are established and the needs of the clientele served by the department identified. In the annual plan of activities and semester assignment, the needs of the department's clientele are addressed through the teaching, research, service and professional practice activities of the faculty.

Faculty recordkeeping, the second step in the development of a faculty recognition system, includes the development of an activities card file and a samples file. The activities card file is a running account of the activities completed by the faculty member during the year. The samples file is a file in which the "products", e.g., journal articles, research proposals, student evaluations, etc., that result from the teaching, research, service and professional practice activity of the faculty member are stored.

Reporting faculty accomplishments, the last step in the process, includes the development of a report of the faculty member's achievements and the preparation of a curriculum vitae and promotion dossier. The annual achievement report complements the annual plan of activities and summarizes the accomplishments of the faculty member for the past year. The currciulum

4

vitae is a complete record of the teaching, research, service and professional practice activities of the faculty member. The promotion dossier documents the faculty member's activities from the time of initial employment or last promotion. It is the major document used in the promotion process.

Each of the documents mentioned above is discussed in detail in the succeeding chapters.

Figure 1.2 illustrates the relationship between the components of the faculty recognition system. The academic department is viewed as the principal administrative unit in the recognition process. The statement of purpose defines the department's philosophic 'raison d'etre' and establishes the parameters that define its perceived areas of responsibility. The goals of the department support the purpose statement and indicate the direction that the department will take in meeting the needs of its clientele. The mission statements written for the areas of teaching, research and scholarly activity, service and professional practice serve to specifically define the types of activities that the department will support.

The social needs, goals, objectives and activities of the faculty within the areas of teaching, research, service and professional practice comprise the operational portion of the system. With the needs of the department's clientele identified and the goals stated, the faculty members then begin working to attain the objectives. Attainment of the objectives by the faculty members are the procedural steps to resolving of the stated needs of the clientele.

The last steps in the faculty recognition process involve the recording and reporting of accomplishments of faculty members as they attain their respective goals and objectives.

Versatility

The faculty recognition system is designed to be used. If a department does not view "Service" as a major area of activity, then the service sections that appear in each of the components of the system should be excluded. If a department faculty thinks "Academic Advisement and Career Counseling" is more appropriately a part of "Department Service" than "Teaching and Related Activities", the advisement and counseling function should be moved under the heading of "Department Service". Or, if a heading has not been included in the examples nor addressed in the chapters, but is viewed by the department as important, it should be entered into the system.

Versatility is one important characteristic of the faculty recognition system. The ability to change the existing structure without destroying the organizational concept, allows a department to adopt the system and modify it to meet its particular needs and those of its faculty members.

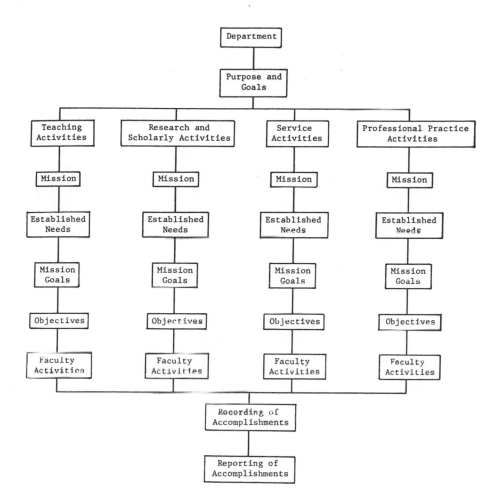

Figure 1.2 - Organizational Structure
of the Faculty Recognition System

DEPARTMENT AND FACULTY
PLANNING

CHAPTER 1

Department Plan

The department plan is a comprehensive plan set forth by the faculty members and chairperson which puts the faculty recognition system into motion. (See Example A.) The plan states the purpose and goals of the department; the department's mission in teaching, research, service and professional practice; the needs of the clientele to be served and the goals for meeting those needs.

The department plan is used for short and long-term planning. It is written for several years into the future (in Example A, the period is five years), but is reviewed annually to note the accomplishments of the past year, update goals that were not attained during that time and set new goals. Reviewing the plan annually reminds the chairperson and faculty members of the commitments of the department and of their individual responsibilities to the department and their own career goals.

The department plan is the single most important resource used by the faculty in preparing their annual plans of activity. (See Chapter Two.) The teaching, research, service and professional practice activities listed in a faculty member's annual plan support the goals for teaching, research, service and professional practice as specified in the department plan. If the annual plans are prepared in the manner suggested in Chapter Two and the faculty members successfully meet their stated goals and objectives, achievement of the purpose and goals of the department is ensured and the basis for recognizing and rewarding faculty performance is established.

Organization

The department plan is introduced by a statement of purpose and list of departmental goals. The purpose and goals statements are followed by the major sections of Teaching and Related Activities, Research and Scholarly Activities, Service Activities and Professional Practice Activities. Each major section is introduced by a mission statement and followed by headings appropriate to the section. Needs of the clientele and goals addressing those needs are included under the various headings.

With minor differences, the basic organizational structure established in the department plan is also found in the annual plan of activities, semester assignment, annual achievement report, curriculum vitae and promotion dossier. The common structure gives the system a needed element of uniformity and provides for continuity between the components.

Purpose

"The purpose of an organization is a statement that defines the relationship of the organizational system to its suprasystem in terms of people and their needs" (Jarett, Rader and Longhurst, 1970, p. 6/03). The purpose is defined in the response to the question, "why does the organization exist?".

In the faculty recognition system, the department is the principal organizational unit. The department's purpose establishes its philosophic 'raison d'etre', identifies the clientele to be served and defines the department's perceived areas of responsibility. The statement of purpose, as taken from the department plan for the Department of Nursing Education, demonstrates application of the above criteria.

> The two-fold purpose of the Department of Nursing Education is to prepare nursing personnel to assist the citizens of Illinois in achieving and maintaining an optimal state of health through the promotion and adoption of sound preventive health care practices and delivery of acute patient care services; and to prepare faculty members for teaching and research positions in nursing education programs.

Goals

The goals of the department immediately follow the statement of purpose in the department plan. As defined by Nervig (1984, p. 3), "goals are statements of broad intent which are general and timeless and not concerned with the measurement of achievement within a specific time period". Appleby (1981) states that "goals give a sense of direction for the activities of an organization. They give *broad* guidelines toward which more detailed and specific plans are directed".[2] Bortz (1981, p. 115) views "a goal as a statement that tells the *direction* [of an organization] . . . and defines the *boundaries within which* [the organization will function]".

The departmental goals shown in Example A respectively indicate the direction the department will take in teaching, research, service and professional practice. By stating the goals in this manner, each category of departmental interest and activity is addressed and the parameters within which the faculty will function are more specifically defined.

---

[2]**Modern Business Administration** (p. 49) by Robert C. Appleby, 1981, London: Pitman, Adapted with permission of publisher.

Mission

"A mission is a narrow form of purpose . . . unique to a particular [function]" (Appleby, 1981).[3] In the department plan, a mission statement introduces the teaching, research, service and professional practice sections. The mission statements support the purpose and goals of the department and define, more specifically, the efforts of the department in each of the four areas. For example, the departmental mission statement, as taken from the Research and Scholarly Activities section of Example A, states how the Department of Nursing Education views its role in research and scholarly activity.

> To contribute to the existing body of knowledge as it pertains to the preparation of nurses, improvement of patient care, nurse education and nursing service; and to ensure the continued growth and development of the faculty and profession, as a whole, through the conduct of research and publication.

The above mission statement supports the broader purpose statement and goals of the department and defines, in more detail, what the department will do to achieve them.

Needs

The needs that appear in the teaching, research, service and professional practice sections of the plan are the needs of the group recognized in the department's purpose statement. The needs are derived from a variety of sources. While the group itself serves as one source of information, individuals and organizations within and outside of the institution provide the majority of the necessary data.

Within the institution, groups constantly study the needs of society and make recommendations as to curricular offerings, programmatic changes or special programs. Deans and chairpersons regularly head efforts to keep their faculties abreast of the needs of their clientele. Private, state and federal agencies, together with professional groups, systematically compile and distribute information to assist university personnel in keeping their programs current.

The social needs addressed by academic institutions are satisfied through teaching, research, service and professional practice. The department plan reflects this organizational approach. The needs of the department's clientele are grouped under headings appropriate to the categories of teaching, research, service and professional practice. In turn, single needs or small groupings of needs serve as the basis for developing the mission goals of the department.

---

[3]Appleby, p. 49.

Linking the needs of the department's clientele to its mission goals is fundamental to the organizational theory of the faculty recognition system. All future activitiy of the department is dependent on the articulation of its mission goals with the educational needs of its clientele.

Mission Goals

A mission goal is a statement of what the department intends to do to meet a single need or small group of needs of its clientele. Unlike a department goal which is a "statement of broad intent . . . general and timeless . . . not concerned with measurement of achievement within a specific time period" (Nervig, 1984, p. 3), a mission goal is more limited in scope.

As shown in the Research portion of the Research and Scholarly Activities section of the department plan, the mission goal is a direct response to two of the needs of the department's clientele. In the annual plan of activities, the mission goal is restated and guides the faculty in defining their objectives for its attainment. (See Chapter Two.)

Content

As discussed above, the content of the department plan is organized in terms of teaching, research, service and professional practice. While the headings used in the four sections have general application to most academic units, they may have to be modified somewhat to meet the specific needs of individual departments. For practical reasons, the following discussions focus on examples that have more generic application.

Teaching and Related Activities

Teaching and related activities are those activities performed by faculty members which relate directly to the "teaching-learning" process or support and enhance it. The headings used to organize the content reflect the sequence of activities found in the mission statement. Teaching students is central to the department's instructional effort. In support of this primary activity is the recruitment of new and transfer students, academic advisement and career counseling, job placement and follow-up, and advanced and continuing education.

Departmental Mission: The mission statement summarizes what the members of the department view as their responsibility to students in the areas of direct teaching and instructional support. The statement reflects the scope and intent of the programmatic offerings of the department, types and levels of instruction to be delivered and clientele to be served.

Teaching and Instruction: Teaching and instruction includes all of the activities performed by faculty members in guiding and directing the learning of students. It includes the imparting of knowledge and sharing of ideas with students, as well as performing the activities needed to support the direct teaching effort.

Direct teaching includes teaching classroom and/or laboratory courses; directing seminars, practicums and independent study; preparing, administering and grading tests; and evaluating student projects. Advising on the development and writing of themes, research papers, theses and dissertations is also considered a part of direct teaching.

Teaching support encompasses such activities as preparing and developing learning materials and instructional aids; writing course materials; and reading, reviewing and revising written materials in preparation for classroom/laboratory instruction. Such activities as the procurement, set-up and maintenance of laboratory apparatus and the ordering of materials and supplies are also considered teaching support.

Other types of activities that can be included in the teaching and instruction portion of the department plan are coaching athletics, directing drama, musical or theatrical groups, monitoring language or scientific laboratories, sponsoring student groups, etc.

Recruitment: Recruitment is the process of bringing new and transfer students to the campus and department. It entails identifying potential students, presenting the educational benefits offered by the institution and department, securing the students' applications for admission and assisting them in gaining admittance.

Activities that the faculty members perform in support of the actual recruitment of students are also a part of the process. Such activities include the development of recruiting materials, setting up of on and off-campus programs, compiling lists of potential students, etc.

Academic Advisement and Career Counseling: Academic advisement is the term reserved specifically for aiding students in planning their academic programs. Implied is a more immediate and limited exchange of information relating to the student's entry into, progress in and successful completion of the academic program. Included in the advisement function is making the students aware of the program, assisting in the selection of courses, monitoring student progress, maintaining student records and assisting students in meeting graduation requirements.

In contrast to academic advisement, career counseling suggests a more extensive and on-going process. In a career counseling role, the faculty members help students explore and evaluate their thoughts and feelings regarding their career aspirations and choice of occupation.

Job Placement and Follow-Up: Job placement is a service extended by the department (or college/university) to its graduates to assist them in finding employment. Follow-up is the activity of keeping up-to-date records of the graduates with regard to types and areas of employment, employment responsibilities, career mobility, additional education, and the like.

Advanced Education: Opportunity for education and training beyond the baccalaureate degree is addressed in this section of the department plan. It directs the efforts of the faculty toward meeting the needs of the department's clientele for graduate study and in-service adult and continuing education.

Research and Scholarly Activities

Research can be defined as a process of systematic inquiry resulting in the acquisition of new knowledge or the verifying or refuting of existing knowledge. Scholarly activity, in turn, can be viewed as the tangible results of a research effort, such as the writing and publishing of journal articles, monographs and books, and/or the preparation and presentation of scholarly papers or such creative works as exhibits, artistic performances and the like.

Departmental Mission: The mission statement of the research and scholarly activities section of the department plan specifies the areas of research and types of scholarly and creative activities encouraged by the department. The statement defines the types of activities that the department will support in meeting the research related needs of its clientele and in contributing to the body of knowledge of the profession/discipline.

The three types of activity included in the departmental mission statement in Example A are research, publications and papers/presentations. Depending on the department, other areas of inquiry and activity can be included. For instance, in a department of music or theater, the study and creative work associated with the fine or performing arts would appropriately be addressed in the research and scholarly activities section of the personnel plan.

Research: This section of the department plan identifies areas of research that the department will address in meeting the research-related needs of its clientele. The statements of need broadly define the problem areas requiring formalized study. The mission goal is the department's initial response to meeting the expressed need(s).

The research section of Example A shows a need for information regarding the education and employment of nurses and an increased awareness of the department's research center. The department's response is a broadly conceived mission goal: ". . . to increase the department's research effort in nursing education . . ." at all levels of activity.

Publications: Publishing serves two ends: to contribute to the body of knowledge of the profession/discipline and to share information with others in the field for purposes of application. Types of publications include books, chapters in books, book reviews, journal articles, monographs, research reports, proceedings papers and abstracts. Other types of publications are newsletters, newspaper articles, brochures and pamphlets, and articles in popular magazines.

The publications which receive highest academic acclaim are peer-reviewed, research-based books and journal articles. Publications which are less theoretical and more practical in nature usually receive somewhat less academic recognition. Publications for public consumption receive the least amount of scholarly acclaim.

Papers/Presentations: Reading scholarly papers and giving presentations in less formal settings are other ways faculty members communicate with their peers and the clientele they serve. As with publications, papers and presentations which are research-based usually receive more recognition for scholarly contribution than do papers and presentations of a more practical nature.

Service Activities

"Service within the academic community may be defined as any effort of the faculty which goes on apart from their specific teaching assignments or particular research endeavors" (Morrill and Spees, 1982, p. 182). Service is defined as the faculty members' offers of assistance to individuals and groups within and outside of the institution who want and can benefit from their specialized knowledge, skill and experience.

Departmental Mission: The departmental mission statement, as it pertains to faculty service and contribution, addresses individuals and groups to be served by the department and the types of service that the department will render. In Example A, the mission of the department is to ". . . assist (people) from the university, the profession and local, state, national and international communities . . . in the areas of education, professional and institutional development and community assistance."

Service to the Institution: Service to the institution is defined as service provided by faculty members to the department, college, university or other units of the institution. It includes, but is not limited to, membership on standing and ad hoc committees; coordination of special programs; participation in institutionally-sponsored conferences, institutes, clinics and workshops; support and guidance of student groups and special assignments representing the institution.

Professional Service: A faculty member's active support of and direct involvement in the organizations and activities of the profession constitutes professional service. Membership in professional organizations, on special committees or on an editorial review board of a professional journal, are examples of service to the profession.

Professional service also includes paid or unpaid consulting work.

Community Service: Community service is the service rendered by the faculty member as a representative of the department, college or institution to individuals and organizations in the local, regional, state, national and international communities. Types of community service range from membership on a local high school advisory committee to establishing a joint Master's degree program between the department and an institution in the Caribbean.

Administration: In most academic situations, the chairperson is the only officially recognized administrator in the department. However, faculty members often assume the roles of coordinator, supervisor, manager, or director in the department or college and perform the administrative duties associated with the titles. The duties, when performed by faculty members as a part of their academic assignments, are normally considered service contributions.

By viewing the administrative duties performed by faculty members as service, the problems associated with adding another major category of activity, i.e. Administration, to the faculty recognition system are avoided. The system is kept in its simplest format and the administrative contributions of the faculty to the department, college or institution are readily legitimatized and recognized.

Professional Development: Professional development encompasses the variety of activities performed by faculty members to keep abreast of new ideas and changes in their discipline or area of professional interest. Such activities include keeping an up-to-date professional reading list, attending seminars and workshops which address new or evolving topics in the field, planning sabbaticals which add to professional growth, securing mini-grants and other funding which support growth in the discipline or profession, and participating in study tours. Any activity which increases a faculty member's knowledge, as it relates to the discipline and profession, qualifies as professional development.

Professional Practice Activities

Professional practice is defined as recognized involvement on the part of faculty members in the practice of their professional specialties while in the employ of the academic institution. One example would be a law professor actively working in a law firm while teaching law and doing scholarly research at a university. Another example would be an engineering professor who assumes faculty responsibilities and, at the same time, works as a consulting engineer to a local industry.

In Example A, two types of professional practice activities are addressed: clinical practice and administrative practice. For nursing education, these two categories are appropriate. However, for professional practice activities in other fields of endeavor different categories of activity might have to be selected.

As with other sections of the department plan, the professional practice section is introduced by a mission statement. It is followed by categories of activity introduced by statements of need and concluded with mission goals addressing the needs.

As mentioned earlier, the professional practice section of the department plan is included for those departments which encourage their faculties to continue a professional practice while assuming their academic responsibilities. However, if professional practice beyond the academic assignment is not supported by the faculty, then this section would not be included in the department plan or any of the subsequent documents of the faculty recognition system.

EXAMPLE A

Department Plan

1986-1991

Department of Nursing Education

College of Applied Science

Southern University

I. DEPARTMENTAL PURPOSE AND GOALS

A. **Purpose:** The two-fold purpose of the Department of Nursing Education is to prepare nursing personnel to assist the citizens of Illinois in achieving and maintaining an optimal state of health through the promotion and adoption of sound preventive health care practices and delivery of acute patient care services; and to prepare faculty members for teaching and research positions in nursing education programs.

B. **Departmental Goals:** The goals of the department reflect the faculty's interest in and concern for collective and individual involvement in the areas of teaching, research, service and professional practice. The goals are to:

1. Prepare undergraduate students for generalist nursing positions and graduate students for teaching, administration or clinical specialty positions in public and private health care delivery agencies;

2. Contribute to the growing body of knowledge as it applies to nursing theory and practice through research and publication;

3. Provide service, as it pertains to nursing education, to individuals; the college and university; the nursing profession; and local, state, national and international public and private organizations; and

4. Encourage faculty to keep their knowledge and skills current in their areas of professional practice.

II. TEACHING AND RELATED ACTIVITIES

A. **Departmental Mission:** The mission of the Department of Nursing Education, as it pertains to teaching and instructional support, is to continue serving the students and profession by providing the following: teaching and instruction necessary to the preparation of qualified nurses and nursing education faculty; recruitment of new students to the department; academic advisement and career counseling to new and continuing students; job placement and follow-up; and advanced and continuing education.

B. **Teaching and Instruction**
Established Needs:
1. Continuing supply of qualified nurses.

2. Inservice education and training for employed nurses.

Mission Goal #1:
Continue delivery of on-campus and off-campus degree granting and continuing education (non-degree granting) programs.

Established Need:
1. Upgrading of skills of nursing support personnel.

Mission Goal #2:
Develop an educational program for nursing support personnel in local health care delivery agencies.

C. **Recruitment:**
Established Needs:
1. An average of 50 B.S.N. graduates per year for employment in local health care delivery agencies.

2. An average of 10 M.S.N. and D.N.Sc. graduates per year for employment in local health care delivery agencies and nursing education programs.

Mission Goal #1:
Increase recruitment of both new and transfer undergraduate and graduate students to on-campus Baccalaureate, Master's and Doctoral degree programs.

Established Need:
1. Maintain the number of nurses currently employed in local health care delivery agencies at 90% (10% attrition rate).

Mission Goal #2:
Provide 24 hours of continuing education programs per year in accordance with evaluated needs.

Established Need:
1. An average of 40 nurses per year needed for employment in the Mt. Vernon and Belleville areas.

Mission Goal #3:
Consider the establishment of an off-campus residence center to service the Mt. Vernon/Belleville areas.

D. **Academic Advisement and Career Counseling**
Established Needs:
1. Increased student and faculty understanding of the undergraduate program and the constraints that affect it.

2. Increased student and faculty understanding of the graduate program and the constraints that affect it.

Mission Goal #1:
Make the faculty and students aware of the current advisement policies and practices of the department and keep them abreast of changes as they arise.

Established Need:
1. Increase in the availability of advisement and career counseling services.

Mission Goal #2:
Continue and expand the advisement and career counseling program for all students in the department.

E. Job Placement and Follow-Up
Established Needs:
1. Increased public awareness of the Department of Nursing Education's capabilities and offerings.
2. Increased employer awareness of career interests and capabilities of program graduates.

Mission Goal #1:
Develop a public relations plan for the department.

Established Needs:
1. All nursing care needs being met by qualified nurses.
2. A pool of qualified nurses to meet employment needs created by attrition and emergency situations.

Mission Goal #2:
Increase the number of job placements for department graduates by 1988 from 65% to 75%.

Established Need:
1. Complete employment data on employed nurses.

Mission Goal #3:
Maintain a current record of all department graduates.

F. Advanced Education
Established Need:
1. Need for nursing personnel with advanced education in nursing theory and practice.

Mission Goal #1:
Continue delivery of on-campus and off-campus graduate and adult and continuing education programs.

III. RESEARCH AND SCHOLARLY ACTIVITIES
A. **Departmental Mission:** The mission of the Department of Nursing Education in the area of research and scholarly activity is two-fold: to contribute to the existing body of knowledge as it pertains to the preparation of nurses, improvement of patient care, nurse education and nursing service; and to ensure the continued growth and development of the faculty and profession, as a whole, through the conduct of research and publication.

B. **Research**
Established Needs:
1. Information as it pertains to the education and employment needs of nurses.

2. Increased public awareness of the department's activities as a nursing education research center.

Mission Goal #1:
Increase the department's research effort in nursing education locally, statewide, nationally and internationally.

C. **Publications**
Established Needs:
1. Nursing related education materials, i.e., textbooks, student guides, individualized instruction, etc.

2. Professional growth and development materials.

Mission Goal #1:
Increase the textbook and journal article publication efforts of **all** faculty members in the department.

D. **Papers/Presentations**
Established Needs:
1. Information as it pertains to the theory and practice of nursing.

2. Information as it pertains to the theory and practice of nursing education.

Mission Goal #1:
Increase faculty involvement and participation in conventions, professional meetings, legislation hearings, etc.

IV. SERVICE ACTIVITIES

A. **Departmental Mission:** The mission of the Department of Nursing Education, as it pertains to service and professional contribution, is to assist individuals and groups from the university, the profession, and local, state, national and international communities who need and seek help in the areas of nursing education and practice, professional and institutional development, and community information and assistance.

B. **Service to the Institution**
   Established Need:
   1. Leadership and assistance in the policy-making, advisory and implementation activities of the institution.

   Mission Goal #1:
   Continue service to the department, college and university.

C. **Professional Service**
   Established Needs:
   1. Support and assistance to public local, state and national nursing and education organizations, i.e., professional associations, certification boards, accrediting bodies, etc.

   2. Support and assistance to private sector organizations.

   Mission Goal #2:
   Continue and expand service to the nursing profession, nursing education organizations, and public and private sector institutions.

   Established Need:
   1. Support and assistance to institutions and organizations outside of the United States.

   Mission Goal #3:
   Continue and expand nursing education-related service to developing countries.

D. **Community Service**
   Established Needs:
   1. Increased public awareness to problems resulting from alcohol and drug abuse.

   2. Reduction of teen-age pregnancies.

   Mission Goal #1:
   Increase local and regional service efforts in areas of specified needs.

E. **Administration**
   Established Need:
   1. Faculty leadership and administrative assistance in carrying out activities in the university, college and/or department.

   Mission Goal #1:
   Assist the administrations of the university, college and/or department to coordinate and implement activities important to their respective units.

F. **Professional Development**
   Established Need:
   1. Faculty members who are abreast of changes, innovations and new insights in the general field of nursing and in their particular specialty areas.

   Mission Goal #1:
   Encourage and recognize the efforts of the faculty to increase their knowledge and skill in the areas of direct client care, nursing education and/or health care administration.

V. PROFESSIONAL PRACTICE ACTIVITIES

A. **Departmental Mission:** The mission of the Department of Nursing Education, as it pertains to professional practice, is to encourage and support the efforts of faculty members to keep their knowledge and skills current in their clinical or administrative specialty areas.

B. **Clinical Practice**
   Established Need:
   1. Faculty members who have current, first-hand experience in their clinical specialty areas.

   Mission Goal #1:
   Encourage and assist members of the Nursing Education faculty to keep current in their clinical specialty areas through direct participation in the clinical setting.

C. **Administrative Practice**
   Established Need:
   1. Faculty members who have current, first-hand experience in their administrative specialty areas.

   Mission Goal #1:
   Encourage and assist members of the Nursing Education faculty to remain current through direct experience in their administrative specialty area.

CHAPTER 2

Annual Plan of Activities

For faculty members in institutions of higher education, the basis for receiving salary increments, merit pay, tenure and promotion is **documentation** of teaching, research, service and professional practice activity. For individual faculty members, preparation of an annual plan of activities begins the documentation process.

The annual plan of activities is an agreement between the faculty member and department chairperson as to the teaching, research, service and professional practice activities of the faculty member for an academic or calendar year. (See Example B.) Reflecting the organization and content of the department plan, the annual plan is the means used by faculty members to define their objectives for the year and align them with the mission goals of the department.

The annual plan is tailored to complement the teaching, research, service and professional practice interests of the faculty member. Once prepared, it guides the department chairperson in making the faculty member's semester or quarterly assignments. (See Chapter Three.)

Organization

The organizational structure of the annual plan parallels that of the department plan. As with the department plan, the annual plan is introduced by the purpose and goals of the department and the sections of Teaching and Related Activities, Research and Scholarly Activities, Service Activities and Professional Practice Activities. Each section is introduced by the mission statement that originally appeared in the department plan.

Content

The content of the annual plan is an extension of the department plan. The headings under the major section titles include a restatement of the mission goals from the department plan, the objectives of the faculty member to meet the stated goals, completion date for attaining the objectives, and resources for their implementation.

Objective

An objective is a specific statement of what the faculty member will do to support a given mission goal. It is an observable activity that results in a tangible product or service. The objective is introduced by a verb and followed by a statement that more specifically describes the action.

In the Research and Scholarly Activities section, the mission goal for research is addressed in the objective: "Seek funding to examine relationships between self-concept and health-seeking behaviors". The objective supports, in part, the broader mission goal of the department and directs the faculty member's research effort in a direction of personal interest and professional expertise.

Completion Date

The completion date for the objective specifies the amount of time required to attain the objective. The date may be changed by consent of the faculty member and chairperson should the situation demand it.

The completion date may or may not fall within the time frame of the annual plan. If it extends beyond the end of the academic or calendar year, the objective would be included in the succeeding annual plan.

Resources

Resources includes all of the human, technical and financial assistance needed by the faculty member to attain the objective. Secretarial assistance, graduate student assistance, duplication services, funding for travel, telephone and computer time, are typical examples of resource items.

One of the responsibilities of the chairperson is to determine if the department can provide the resources needed by the faculty to attain their proposed objectives. If the resources are not available in the department, outside sources will have to be identified. If no outside assistance is available, the faculty members will have to modify their plans to accommodate the department's capability to support their activities.

Agreement

The agreement section of the annual plan of activities represents an understanding of and agreement between the chairperson and faculty member as to the latter's plan of activity for the academic or calendar year. Any amendment to the proposed plan requires the consent of both parties.

The agreement is formalized with the dated signatures of the chairperson and faculty member.

Adaptability

By design, the annual plan of activities is narrower in scope and purpose than the department plan. An individual's annual plan is not intended to address all of the mission goals presented in the department plan. Rather, it is the means by which faculty members focus their energies on activities that support the purpose and goals of the department and, at the same time, move them toward their career and professional goals.

Also, the annual plan of activities can be changed as circumstances change. When this occurs, the faculty member and chairperson meet to discuss amendment of the current plan. A new objective may be added to the appropriate section of the annual plan or substituted for one that is already in place. Assuming that the annual plan defines a "full load" for the faculty member, the latter approach is more desirable.

Care must be taken when modifying an existing annual plan. Does the new objective support the department effort? Does its inclusion in the plan retain an acceptable balance of teaching, research, service and professional practice activity for the faculty member? Is the proposed objective as equitable in terms of time, work requirements, and needed resources as the present objective? Can the change be made without unduly affecting the department or the schedules and activities of other faculty members? If the proposed objective is added to the current list of objectives of the annual plan, will the amount of work required to attain it be too much for the faculty member? Before making any changes in the faculty member's annual plan, questions such as these must be addressed.

EXAMPLE B

Annual Plan of Activities

for

Dr. Frances Keen

Associate Professor

1986-87

Department of Nursing Education

College of Applied Science

Southern University

I. DEPARTMENTAL PURPOSE AND GOALS

A. **Purpose:** The two-fold purpose of the Department of Nursing Education is to prepare nursing personnel to assist the citizens of Illinois in achieving and maintaining an optimal state of health through the promotion and adoption of sound preventive health care practices and delivery of acute patient care services; and to prepare faculty members for teaching and research positions in nursing education programs.

B. **Departmental Goals:** The goals of the department reflect the faculty's interest in and concern for collective and individual involvement in the areas of teaching, research, service and professional practice. The goals are to:

1. Prepare undergraduate students for generalist nursing positions and graduate students for teaching, administration or clinical specialty positions in public and private health care delivery agencies;

2. Contribute to the growing body of knowledge as it applies to nursing theory and practice through research and publication;

3. Provide service, as it pertains to nursing education, to individuals; the college and university; the nursing profession; and local, state, national and international public and private organizations; and

4. Encourage faculty to keep their knowledge and skills current in their areas of professional practice.

II. TEACHING AND RELATED ACTIVITIES

A. **Departmental Mission:** The mission of the Department of Nursing Education, as it pertains to teaching and instructional support, is to continue serving the students and profession by providing the following: teaching and instruction necessary to the preparation of qualified nurses and nursing education faculty; recruitment of new students to the department; academic advisement and career counseling to new and continuing students; job placement and follow-up; and advanced and continuing education.

B. **Areas of Specialization/Interests**
    1. Medical-surgical nursing
    2. Transcultural nursing

C. **Teaching and Instruction**
    Mission Goal #1
        Continue delivery of on-campus and off-campus degree granting programs and continuing education (non-degree granting) programs.

        Objective #1—Continue delivery of NE 360 - Adult Health Nursing I and NE 460 - Adult Health Nursing II.

Completion Date: The semester the course assignments are made. NE 460—Two week concentrated delivery, summer, 1986.

Resources—Financial support for development of new materials and updating of existing ones.

Objective #2—Deliver an in-service workshop in critical-care nursing in Chicago, Rockford, Metro-East St. Louis and Centralia.

Completion Date: End of summer, 1987.

Resources—Finances for travel, per diem, development of workshop materials and graduate assistance.

Objective #3—Establish a competency-based nursing assistant program.

Completion Date: End of 1986-87 academic year.

Resources—Release time 25% during academic year; 50% during summers. Financial assistance for purchase of needed materials, developmental costs, travel and per diem, consultant's fees, graduate assistance and secretarial help.

D. **Recruitment**
   Mission Goal #1
   Increase recruitment of both new and transfer undergraduate and graduate students to on-campus Baccalaureate, Master's and Doctoral degree programs.

   Objective #1—Recruit 6-8 new/transfer students to the Baccalaureate Nursing program.

   Completion Date: End of Spring Semester, 1986.

   Resources—Finances for travel, per diem; regional list of potential sources for students.

   Mission Goal #3
   Consider the establishment of an off-campus residence center to service the Mt. Vernon/Belleville areas.

   Objective #2—Assist in the conduct of a feasibility study of the need for a residence center in the Mt. Vernon/Belleville areas. areas.

   Completion Date: End of the 1986-87 academic year.

Resources—Feasibility study committee; financial support for additional graduate student assistance and secretarial help, duplication, computer time.

E. **Academic Advisement and Career Counseling**
    Mission Goal #1
    Make the faculty and students aware of the current advisement policies and practices of the department and keep them abreast of changes as they arise

   Objective #1—Write a Student/Advisor's Guide for the Baccalaureate Nursing program.

   Completion Date: End of Summer Semester, 1986.

   Resources—Set of current advisement materials; access to department advisors.

   Objective #2—Conduct a faculty-student survey as to the perceived need for an advisement and career counseling center.

   Completion Date: End of Summer Semester, 1986.

   Resources—List of names and addresses of currently enrolled students and department graduates; secretarial help; computer time.

III. RESEARCH AND SCHOLARLY ACTIVITIES

   A. **Departmental Mission:** The mission of the Department of Nursing Education in the area of research and scholarly activity is two-fold: to contribute to the existing body of knowledge as it pertains to the preparation of nurses, improvement of patient care, nurse education and nursing service; and to ensure the continued growth and development of the faculty and profession, as a whole, through the conduct of research and publication.

   B. **Areas of Specialization/Interests**
       1. Medical-surgical nursing
       2. Transcultural nursing

C. Research

Mission Goal #1

Increase the department's research effort in nursing education locally, statewide, nationally and internationally.

Objective #1—Seek funding to examine relationships between self-concept and health-seeking behaviors.

Completion Date: June 30, 1987.

Resources—Secretarial help, graduate assistance (all costs of project to be assumed by same).

Objective #2—Seek funding to establish a Master of Science in Nursing degree with a specialty in tropical disease nursing.

Completion Date: End of 1986 academic year.

Resources—Secretarial assistance, department faculty assistance, travel expense monies.

D. **Publications**
Mission Goal #1

Increase the textbook and journal article publication efforts of **all faculty** members in the department.

Objective #1—Complete a journal manuscript describing Southern University's off-campus extension programs.

Completion Date: December, 1986.

Resources—Secretarial assistance, duplication materials.

E. **Papers/Presentations**

Mission Goal #1

Increase faculty involvement and participation in conventions, professional meetings, legislative hearings, etc.

Objective #1—Present a paper at the National League for Nursing convention.

Completion Date: December, 1986.

Resources—Secretarial assistance, financial assistance to cover costs of duplication.

IV. SERVICE ACTIVITIES

A. **Departmental Mission:** The mission of the Department of Nursing Education, as it pertains to service and professional contribution, is to assist individuals and groups from the university, the profession and local, state, national and international communities who need and seek help in the areas of nursing education and practice, professional and institutional development, and community information and assistance.

B. **Service to the Institution**

Mission Goal #1

Continue service to the department, college and university.

Objective #1—Serve on one standing department committee and one college or university committee.

Completion Date: End of 1986-87 academic year.

Resources—Not applicable.

C. **Professional Service**
Mission Goal #2

Continue and expand nursing education-related service to developing countries.

Objective #1—Assist the College of Technology of the Caribbean, Kingston, Jamaica, in the development of their nursing program.

Completion Date: End of 1987-88 academic year.

Resources—Financial assistance for travel, per diem and purchase of limited numbers of published and unpublished informational materials.

D. **Administration**
Mission Goal #1

Assist the administrations of the university, college and/or department to coordinate and implement activities important to their respective units.

Objective #1—Coordinate the off-campus Nursing Education program at Harrison, Illinois.

Completion Date— On-going.

Resources—Financial assistance for travel and per diem, secretarial/student work assistance.

E. **Professional Development**
   Mission Goal #1

   Encourage and recognize the efforts of the faculty to increase their knowledge and skill in the areas of direct client care, nursing education and/or health care administration.

   Objective #1—Attend the American Association of Critical-Care Nurses National Teaching Institute.

   Completion Date: July 20-23, 1987.

   Resources—Financial assistance for travel and per diem.

   Objective #1—Serve mini-sabbatical at Cook County General Hospital in the critical-care nursing unit.

   Completion Date: Interim, summer, 1986—fall, 1986.

   Resources: Not applicable.

V. PROFESSIONAL PRACTICE ACTIVITIES

A. **Departmental Mission:** The mission of the Department of Nursing Education, as it pertains to professional practice, is to encourage and support the efforts of faculty members to keep their knowledge and skills current in their clinical or administrative specialty areas.

B. **Clinical Practice**
   Mission Goal #1

   Encourage and assist members of the Nursing Education faculty to keep current in their clinical specialty areas through direct participation in the clinical setting.

   Objective #1—Continue the critical-care nursing practice at Memorial Hospital.

   Completion Date: On-going each summer.

   Resources: Not applicable.

VI. AGREEMENT

Both parties understand and agree to the proposed plan of activities for the 1986-87 academic year. Amendment of the plan requires mutual consent of the chairperson and faculty member.

Catherine Roberts   _July 15, 1986_
Chairperson   Date

n. f. hee   _July 17, 1986_
Faculty Member   Date

CHAPTER 3

Semester Assignment

The semester assignment is the form used by the chairperson to make semester (or quarterly) assignments to faculty members. (See Example C.) The assignment form continues the process of documenting the teaching, research, service and professional practice activities of the faculty member on a term-by-term basis.

The assignment form is prepared by the chairperson and given to the faculty member prior to the semester or quarter for which the assignment is being made. The dated signature of the chairperson concludes the form.

Organization

The organizational structure of the assignment form reflects the structure established in the department plan and continued in the annual plan of activities. The four major headings are Teaching and Related Activities, Research and Scholarly Activities, Service Activities and Professional Practice Activities.

Content

The content of the semester assignment is derived from the objectives stated in the annual plan of activities prepared by the faculty member. For example, the research proposal regarding "self-concept and health-seeking behaviors" first addressed in the annual plan now appears as the faculty member's semester research assignment.

The planning and continuity initiated at the department level have now been extended to the operational stage to be carried out by the faculty member.

EXAMPLE C

Semester Assignment

for

Dr. Frances Keen

Associate Professor

Department of Nursing Education

College of Applied Science

Southern University

Semester Assignment

Faculty Member: Dr. Frances Keen

In conjunction with your 1986-87 Annual Plan of Activities, your assignment for the Spring Semester, 1987 is as follows:

I. TEACHING AND RELATED ACTIVITIES
   A. NE 460 - Adult Health Nursing II 20%
   B. Recruitment - B.S.N. Program 5%
   C. In-service workshops 10%
   D. Student/Advisor's Guide 15%
   Sub-total 50%

II. RESEARCH AND SCHOLARLY ACTIVITIES

   A. Proposal - Self-concept 20%
   Sub-total 20%

III. SERVICE ACTIVITIES

   A. Department Curriculum Committee 5%
   B. Chair, Intercollegiate Athletic Committee 5%
   C. Coordinator, Harrison program 20%
   Sub-total 30%

IV. PROFESSIONAL PRACTICE ACTIVITIES

   A. No Spring Semester assignment 0%
   Sub-total 0%

   TOTAL 100%

If you have any questions regarding the assignment, please call or make an appointment to discuss them with me.

Catherine Roberts _August 17, 1986_
Chairperson   Date

FACULTY RECORDKEEPING

CHAPTER 4

Activities Card File

The activities card file is a cumulative record of a faculty member's teaching, research, service and professional practice activities for an academic or calendar year. It is the means by which faculty members keep a running account of the activities they perform in attaining the objectives specified in their annual plans (see Chapter Two). Also, the card file is used to record activities performed by the faculty member during the year, but which are not directed at pre-planned objectives.

Figure 4.1 shows an activities card file.

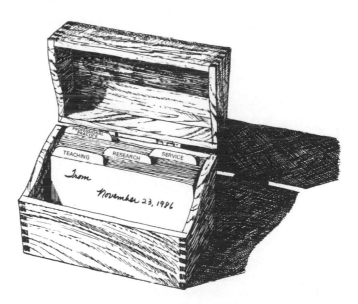

Figure 4.1 - Activities
Card File

Organization

The card file is organized into four major sections: Teaching and Related Activities, Research and Scholarly Activities, Service Activities and Professional Practice Activities. Depending on the faculty member, index cards with sub-headings corresponding to those at the major sections may also be used.

Content

The activities card file is introduced by a date card. See Figure 4.2. The entry on the card indicates the starting date of the card file. Once the information

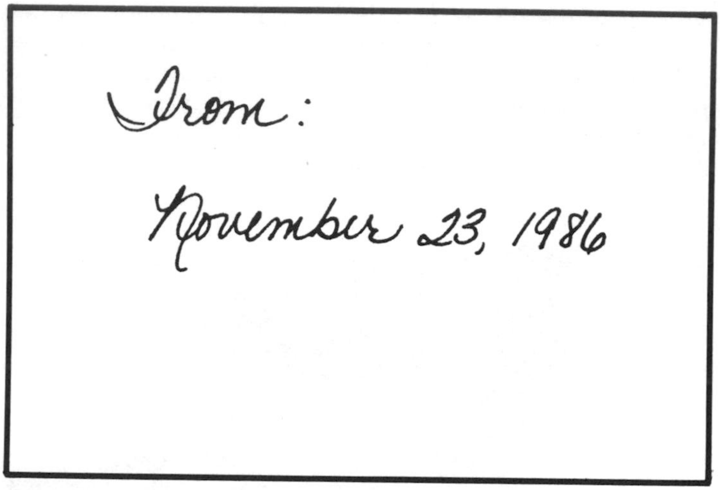

From:

November 23, 1986

Figure 4.2 - Date Card
with Entry

on the set of file cards is used to update the faculty member's curriculum vitae (see Chapter Seven), a new date card is prepared to mark the beginning of another recording cycle.

The content of a completed file card reflects the organizational structure established in the faculty member's annual plan. See Figure 4.3. The card is introduced by the heading appropriate to the activity being reported, the objective for which the activity has been completed, the progress statement and date of completion.

```
Heading:    Research
Objective:  Seek funding for
            Self-Concept/Health-
            Seeking Behaviors
            Study

Progress:   Completed proposal

Completion
    Date:   October 16, 1986
```

Figure 4.3 - Completed Activities
File Card

For an activity that is not directed toward the attainment of a pre-planned objective, but has been performed by the faculty member, the recording process varies only slightly. The heading of the section appropriate to the activity is entered on the file card followed by the activity and its completion date. No objective is included in this latter situation.*

Recording

Maintaining a current activities card file demands constant attention. Care must be taken to record the activities promptly and accurately. By including the appropriate information on the file cards, the activities of the faculty member will articulate with the objectives specified in his/her annual plan.

Later, the same file cards will assist the faculty member in preparing an annual achievement report. (See Chapter Six.)

---

* If the annual plan does not have an appropriate heading, a new one is introduced and later included in the "Additional Activities" section of the annual achievement report. (See Chapter Six.)

CHAPTER 5

Samples File

As faculty members complete their teaching, research, service and professional practice activities during the year, a variety of "products" in the form of journal articles, research reports, course-instructor evaluation forms, presentation papers, class materials, etc. result. A samples file is one effective way of organizing and safely storing these materials. Later, the materials will be used in documenting the faculty member's activities for purposes of evaluation. Figure 5.1 shows a samples file.

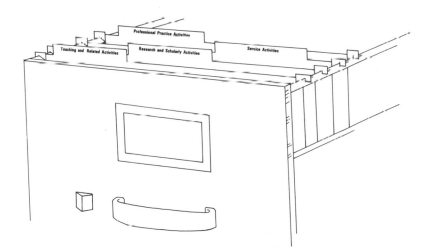

Figure 5.1 - Samples File

Organization

Reflecting the organization of the annual plan, the samples file includes the sections of Teaching and Related Activities, Research and Scholarly Activities, Service Activities, and Professional Practice Activities. Where appropriate, tabbed file folders are included within the hanging files for specific types of documents. See Figure 5.2. Also, a file folder tabbed "Forms" can be included to hold the department plan, annual plan of activities, semester assignments, annual achievement report and curriculum vitae.

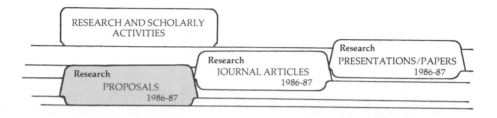
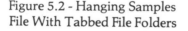

Figure 5.2 - Hanging Samples
File With Tabbed File Folders

Content

Figure 5.3 shows the entries on the tab of a file folder. The folder is one of several folders that might appear in the "Research and Scholarly Activities"

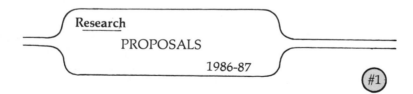

Figure 5.3 - File Folder
Entries

samples file. The tab is introduced by the title of the heading "Research" followed by the types of items included in the folder (in this case, "Proposals") and the academic or calendar year for which the file is being kept.

In Figure 5.3, the #1 on the front of the file folder indicates its order in the sequence of folders in the Research and Scholarly Activities samples file. The number is written on the file to help maintain the order of the folders within the hanging file.

REPORTING FACULTY ACCOMPLISHMENTS

CHAPTER 6

Annual Achievement Report

The annual achievement report is a detailed summary of a faculty member's teaching, research, service and professional practice activities for an academic or calendar year. (See Example D.) The report documents the success of a faculty member in attaining the goals and objectives specified in his/her annual plan of activities.

When used in concert with the annual plan, the achievement report becomes the basis for assessing the faculty member's performance. The annual plan outlines the proposed activities of the faculty member for a particular year. The achievement report summarizes the accomplishments of the faculty member for that same period of time. (A detailed discussion of the evaluation process appears in Chapter Nine.)

Organization

The organizational structure of the achievement report reflects that of the annual plan of activities. The achievement report is introduced by the purpose and goals of the department. It is organized into the major sections of Teaching and Related Activities, Research and Scholarly Activities, Service Activities and Professional Practice Activities. Each section is introduced by the mission statement that appeared in the annual plan. The headings within each section also appear in both documents.

Content

The content of the achievement report also reflects the content of the annual plan. Although the mission goals are absent from the report, the objectives of the faculty member, with their respective completion dates, are included.

Unlike the annual plan, the achievement report includes a "progress" statement. These statements indicate the degree of success realized by the faculty member in attaining the objectives. The statements mark attainment of the objective in total, partial attainment of the objective or no evidence of progress.

Additional Activities

The teaching, research, service and professional practice activities performed by the faculty member during the year, but not included in his/her annual plan, are referred to as "additional activities." In many instances, the activities do not merit amending the annual plan, but should be recognized as a part of the faculty member's total contribution.

As the additional activities are completed, they are entered in the activities card file. Any "products" which result from completion of the activities are placed in the samples file. At the end of the academic or calendar year, the activities are listed under the appropriate headings in the "Additional Activities" section of the annual achievement report. (See Example D.)

Completion

The completion statement concludes the annual achievement report. The statement verifies attainment of or the degree of progress toward the teaching, research, service and professional practice objectives initially specified in the annual plan.

The statement is formalized with the signature of the faculty member and the date of signing.

Example D

Annual Achievement Report

for

Dr. Frances Keen

Associate Professor

1986-87

Department of Nursing Education

College of Applied Science

Southern University

I. DEPARTMENTAL PURPOSE AND GOALS

A. **Purpose:** The two-fold purpose of the Department of Nursing Education is to prepare nursing personnel to assist the citizens of Illinois in achieving and maintaining an optimal state of health through the promotion and adoption of sound preventive health care practices and delivery of acute patient care services; and to prepare faculty members for teaching and research positions in nursing education programs.

B. **Departmental Goals:** The goals of the department reflect the faculty's interest in and concern for collective and individual involvement in the areas of teaching, research, service and professional practice. The goals are to:

1. Prepare undergraduate students for generalist nursing positions and graduate students for teaching, administration or clinical specialty positions in public and private health care delivery agencies;

2. Contribute to the growing body of knowledge as it applies to nursing theory and practice through research and publication;

3. Provide service, as it pertains to nursing education, to individuals; the college and university; the nursing profession; and local, state, national and international public and private organizations; and

4. Encourage faculty to keep their knowledge and skills current in their areas of professional practice.

II. TEACHING AND RELATED ACTIVITIES

A. **Departmental Mission:** The mission of the Department of Nursing Education, as it pertains to teaching and instructional support, is to continue serving the students and profession by providing the following: teaching and instruction necessary to the preparation of qualified nurses and nursing education faculty; recruitment of new students to the department; academic advisement and career counseling to new and continuing students; job placement and follow-up; and advanced and continuing education.

B. **Areas of Specialization/Interests**

1. Medical-surgical nursing

2. Transcultural nursing

C. **Teaching and Instruction**

Objective #1 - Continue delivery of NE 360-Adult Health Nursing I and Adult Health Nursing I and NE 460-Adult Health Nursing II.

Completion Date:

1. NE 360-Adult Health Nursing I (fall, 1986).

*2. NE 584-Advanced Techniques in Medical-Surgical Nursing (fall, 1986).

3. NE 460-Adult Health Nursing II (fall, 1986 and spring, 1987).

Progress: All teaching assignments completed satisfactorily.

Special Note:

Teaching Awards and Honors: University Teacher of the Year, Southern University, May, 1986.

Objective #2—Deliver an in-service workshop in critical-care nursing in Chicago, Rockford, Metro-East St. Louis and Centralia.

Completion Date: End of summer, 1987.

Progress:
1. Rockford, May 2, 1986.

2. Metro-East St. Louis, October 26, 1986.

Objective #3—Establish a competency-based nursing assistant program.

Completion Date: End of 1986-87 academic year.

Progress: Completion of occupational analysis. (Phase one of developmental process completed.)

D. **Recruitment**

Objective #1—Recruit 6-8 new/transfer students to the Baccalaureate Nursing program.

Completion Date: End of Spring Semester, 1986.

Progress: Recruited 5 students.

Objective #2—Assist in the conduct of a feasibility study of the need for a residence center in the Mt. Vernon/Belleville area.

Completion Date: End of 1987-88 academic year.

Progress: Developed and fieldtested employer survey instrument.

* New course begun in department.

E. **Academic Advisement and Career Counseling**

Objective #1—Write a Student/Advisor's Guide for the Baccalaureate Nursing program.

Completion Date: End of Summer Session, 1986.

Progress: Completed Student/Advisor's Guide; August, 1986.

Objective #2—Conduct a faculty-student survey as to the perceived need for an advisement and career counseling center.

Completion Date: End of Fall Semester, 1986.

Progress: Survey in final editing stage. Needs to be proofread, duplicated and distributed to faculty for consensus.

III. RESEARCH AND SCHOLARLY ACTIVITIES

A. **Departmental Mission:** The mission of the Department of Nursing Education in the area of research and scholarly activity is two-fold: to contribute to the existing body of knowledge as it pertains to the preparation of nurses, improvement of patient care, nurse education and nurse service; and to insure the continued growth and development of the faculty and profession, as a whole, through the conduct of research and publication.

B. **Areas of Specialization/Interests**

   1. Medical-surgical nursing
   2. Transcultural nursing

C. **Research**

   Objective #1—Seek funding to examine relationships between self-concept and health-seeking behaviors.

   Completion Date: June 30, 1987.

   Progress: Project funded. Developed and pilot-tested written test instruments.

   Objective #2—Seek funding to establish as Master of Science in Nursing degree with a specialty in tropical disease nursing.

   Completion Date: End of 1986 academic year.

   Progress: Will be funded by the World Health Organization. Have begun writing first draft of proposal.

D. Publications

> **Objective #1**—Complete a journal manuscript describing Southern University's off-campus extension programs.
>
> **Completion Date:** December, 1986.
>
> **Progress:** Completed and submitted for publication October, 1986.

E. Papers/Presentations

> **Objective #1**—Present a paper at the National League for Nursing convention.
>
> **Completion Date:** December, 1986.
>
> **Progress:** Presented paper, "Competency-based Education: The New Approach to Preparing Nurses". September 15, 1986.

IV. SERVICE ACTIVITIES

A. **Departmental Mission:** The mission of the Department of Nursing Education, as it pertains to service and professional contribution, is to assist individuals and groups from the university, the profession and local, state, national and international communities who need and seek help in the areas of nursing education and practice, professional and institutional development, and community information and assistance.

B. **Service to the Institution**

> **Objective #1**—Serve on one standing department committee and one college or university committee.
>
> **Completion Date:** End of 1986-87 academic year.
>
> **Progress:**
>
> 1. Department Graduate Affairs Committee.
> 2. Intercollegiate Athletic Committee.

C. **Professional Service**

> **Objective #1**—Assist the College of Technology of the Caribbean, Kingston, Jamaica, in the development of their nursing program.
>
> **Completion Date:** End of 1987-88 academic year.
>
> **Progress:** Planning trip to CTC and to USAID and USIA, Washington, D.C.

D. **Administration**

> **Objective #1**—Coordinate the off-campus Nursing Education program at Harrison, Illinois.

Completion Date: On-going.

Progress:

1. Six out of eight courses already delivered in Cycle I.

2. Spring Semester, 1986 beginning Cycle II.

3. Beginning recruitment for Cycle III.

E. **Professional Development**

Objective #1—Attend the American Association of Critical-Care Nurses National Teaching Institute.

Completion Date: July 20-23, 1987.

Progress: Attended workshop and gained competence in administration of aortic balloon pump therapy.

V. PROFESSIONAL PRACTICE ACTIVITIES

A. **Departmental Mission:** The mission of the Department of Nursing Education, as it pertains to professional practice, is to encourage and support the efforts of faculty members to keep their knowledge and skills current in their clinical or administrative specialty areas.

B. **Clinical Practice**

Objective #1—Continue the critical-care nursing practice at Memorial Hospital.
Completion Date: On-going each summer.

Progress: Satisfactory.

VI. ADDITIONAL ACTIVITIES

A. Teaching and Related Activities

1. Academic Advisement and Career Counseling

a. Advised students at newly-opened residence center at Elizabethville, August, 1986.

B. Research and Scholarly Activities

1. Papers/Presentations

a. Presentation: "The Need for a Faculty Recognition System". College of Liberal Arts and Sciences In-service Day. September, 14, 1986.

C. Service Activities

1. Departmental Service

a. Supervised modernization of the inorganic chemistry

laboratory, Spring Semester, 1987.

VII.   COMPLETION

The above is a report of my teaching, research, service and professional practice activities for the 1986-87 academic year.

_____   _____
Faculty Member   Date

CHAPTER 7

Curriculum Vitae

The curriculum vitae is a complete record of the academic activity of a faculty member. The vitae is a detailed account of the teaching, research, service and professional practice efforts of faculty members throughout their professional lives. (See Example E.)

The vitae serves as the primary resource in the academic promotion process. It provides a categorical listing of the activities of the faculty member and the dates of their occurrence. Another use of the vitae is to inform interested individuals and organizations outside of the academic institution, such as prospective employers and funding agencies, of the faculty member's areas of interest and expertise.*

Organization

The curriculum vitae is introduced by a personal data section, educational history and list of professional experiences. Also included on the first page of the vitae is the date on which the document was prepared.

The personal data section includes the name and title of the faculty member, home address, date and place of birth, Social Security number and current institutional address and telephone number.

The educational history section traces the faculty member's undergraduate and graduate preparation. The section includes the degrees received, names of the institutions awarding the degrees, graduation dates and academic majors or areas of specialization.

The professional experiences section includes a description of the faculty member's present assignment and prior professional assignments at other academic institutions and/or public or private organizations.

---

* An abbreviated curriculum vitae (1-3 pages) can be substituted in situations where a total document is inappropriate or not needed. A complete vitae can be supplied by the faculty member at a later time if a more detailed profile is requested.

The date that appears on the curriculum vitae indicates the last time that the vitae was updated. The date on the vitae corresponds to the date on the date card in the activities card file. (See Chapter Four.) This date marks the time at which the data from the activities card file was transferred to the vitae.

Content

As with each of the preceding documents in the faculty recognition system, the curriculum vitae is organized into four major sections: Teaching and Related Activities, Research and Scholarly Activities, Service Activities and Professional Practice Activities.

Teaching and Related Activities

The Teaching and Related Activities section is introduced by the areas of specialization of the faculty member as they pertain to teaching and followed by a listing of the awards and honors received for meritorious teaching performance. The remaining entries in the section deal with graduate faculty status (may not be appropriate for all institutions) and the chairing of and membership on graduate student committees.

Depending on the policies and practices of individual departments, other entries that might be included in the Teaching and Related Activities section of the vitae are the titles of courses taught, listing of graduate students and the titles of their theses/dissertations.

Research and Scholarly Activities

The Research and Scholarly Activities section of the curriculum vitae is introduced by a statement of research specialization and interests of the faculty member. The introductory statement is followed by the list of research grants and projects in which the faculty member has been involved. Each entry specifies the role of the faculty member on the grant/project, the title of the award and its funding dates.

The publications portion of the Research and Scholarly Activities section is a comprehensive list of publications of the faculty member. As shown in Example E, the entries include books, chapters in books, journal articles, publications under review, research reports and course materials. Papers which have been presented by the faculty member and subsequently published are also presented. Other types of written material which may be appropriately documented as publications are transcripts of proceedings, articles in newspapers and popular magazines, abstracts, book reviews and monographs.

Papers and presentations given by the faculty member conclude the Research and Scholarly Activities section of the curriculum vitae. The presentation entries include the faculty member's name and the date, title and location of the presentations. If other individuals participated in a given presentation, their names also appear in the entry.

Other types of creative work, for example, exhibits, concerts and recitals, stage performances, readings and interpretations, and formal debates are also a part of the Research and Scholarly Activities section of the curriculum vitae. The various activities are included in the section under appropriately descriptive headings.

Service Activities

The Service Activities section of the curriculum vitae includes the faculty member's service contributions to the institution, profession and community. Service to the institution includes service to the department, college and university. In most cases, institutional service is reported as memberships on standing and ad hoc committees, but also includes individual contribution.

Professional service encompasses memberships in professional organizations, appointments to committees and groups that contribute to the well-being of the profession and its members, special recognition of the faculty member's support of the profession and private consulting work.

Community service encompasses those activities that the faculty member provides the community as a representative of the department, college and/or institution. Each community service entry defines the role of the faculty member in the activity, the name or nature of the activity and the date when it took place.

Administration, when performed by faculty members as a part of their assignment to the department, college or university, is viewed as service activity. The entries include the title of the administrative position, title of the unit being served and/or activity being administered, and dates of the assignment.

The last entry in the Service Activities section of the curriculum vitae is professional development. Included are the various activities undertaken by the faculty member to maintain and add to his/her professional knowledge and skill. An entry contains a statement describing the activity and the place and date of its occurrence.

Professional Practice Activities

The Professional Practice Activities section of the curriculum vitae lists the activities completed by the faculty member to increase his/her knowledge and skill in the professional specialty area. The activities are functionally grouped and include a description of the activity, the place where it was performed and the dates of its occurrence.

In each of the above sections, the entries are arranged in descending order with most recent appearing first on the list. The style in which the items are presented remains the choice of the department implementing the faculty recognition system.

Example E

Curriculum Vitae

for

Dr. Frances Keen

Associate Professor

Department of Nursing Education

College of Applied Science

Southern University

I. PERSONAL   November 23, 1986

   A.   Name   Dr. M. Frances Keen

   B.   Home Address   309 Rodger's Forge
                                      Columbus, Illinois 62888

   C.   Date and Place of Birth   June 8, 1949
                                        Lancaster, Pennsylvania

   D.   Social Security Number   000-00-0001

   E.   Present University Unit   Department of Nursing Education
                                        College of Applied Science
                                        Southern University

II. EDUCATIONAL HISTORY

   A.   D.N.Sc.   The University of America   1976   Medical-surgical nursing
                       Washington, D.C.   Nursing education

   B.   M.S.N.   University of Maryland   1973 Nursing
                       Baltimore, Maryland

   C.   B.S.N.   University of Maryland   1971 Nursing
                       Baltimore, Maryland

III. PROFESSIONAL EXPERIENCES

   A. Current Assignment
       1. Associate Professor, Southern University, Columbus, Illinois, August, 1982 to present. Promotion: Spring, 1982.

       2. Member, Graduate Faculty, 1980 to present.

       3. Coordinator, off-campus Nursing Education program, Harrison, Illinois, 1981 to present.

   B. Prior Assignments
       1. Assistant Professor, University of Maryland School of Nursing, Graduate Faculty, Medical-Surgical Nursing, Baltimore, Maryland, August 1976 - June 1978.

       2. Clinical Nurse, Medical-Surgical Float Pool, The Johns Hopkins Hospital, Baltimore, Maryland, January 1975 - June 1976.

       3. Nursing Curriculum Researcher, The Johns Hopkins University School of Hygiene and Public Health, Baltimore, Maryland, January, 1974 - December, 1975. Project Staff, DHEW Grant, "Nursing Curriculum Design to Promote Role Transition".

4. Visiting Nurse, Extended Service Unit, Visiting Nurse Association, Baltimore, Maryland, July - December, 1974.

5. Instructor, The Johns Hopkins University School of Health Services, Nursing Education Program, Baltimore, Maryland, February 1971 - July 1974.

IV. TEACHING AND RELATED ACTIVITIES

A. Areas of Specialization/Interest

1. Medical-surgical nursing

2. Transcultural nursing

B. Teaching Awards and Honors

1. University Teacher of the Year, Southern University, May, 1986.

2. Award of Merit, "The Adult Patient". Learning Materials Category, American Association of Nurse Educators, January, 1983.

3. Distinguished Scholar, Distinguished Scholar Program, Department of Nursing, University of Manitoba, Winnipeg, Manitoba, Canada, July, 1980.

4. Honorary Instructor, Air Medical Command, Brigham AFB, Johnson, North Carolina, April, 1979.

C. Graduate Faculty Status

1. Category I.   Approved to chair doctoral committees.

D. Graduate Program Chairships

1. M.S.N. - 12

2. D.N.Sc. - 7

E. Graduate Program Committee Memberships

1. M.S.N. - 28

2. D.N.Sc. - 12

V. RESEARCH AND SCHOLARLY ACTIVITIES

A. Areas of Specialization/Interest

1. Medical-surgical nursing

2. Transcultural nursing

B. Research

1. Principal Investigator. "A study to examine the relationships between self-concept and health-seeking behaviors". National Institutes of Health. January 1, 1986 through June 30, 1987.

2. Principal Investigator. "Competency-based nursing education project". Illinois Department of Nursing. October 1, 1984 through September 30, 1986.

3. Co-investigator. "Peace corps recruiting grant". ACTION/Peace Corps, Washington, D.C. July 1, 1984 through June 30, 1985 (with Jeanne Fisher).

4. Co-investigator. "Development of a model curriculum for a master's degree level outreach nursing program". National Association of Practicing Nurses. September 1, 1983 through August 30, 1984 (with F. Raisen).

5. Principal Investigator. "Development of an affiliation program between southern university, department of nursing education and college of the caribbean, bridgetown, barbados". January 1, 1980 through December 31, 1981.

6. Principal Investigator. "Author's market study to textbook needs in nursing education". Training Systems Designers. January 1, 1979 through June 30, 1979.

C. Publications:

1. Books
   a. Keen, F. (1985). **Rheumatic disease nursing - a primer.** Carbondale: Training Systems Designers.
   b. Keen, F. and Dunbar, S. (1983). **A suggested program of study for preparing health-care aides.** Atlanta: Gray Press.

2. Chapters in Professional Books
   a. Keen, F. (1983). Nursing as a profession. In W. Leka, **Career guide to medical and health care occupations.** Carbondale: Training Systems Designers.

3. Articles in Professional Journals
   a. Keen, F. (1985). Development of extension programs to meet community needs. **Journal of Nursing Education, 29**(1), 39-41.
   b. Dear, M.R. and Keen, F. (1983). Role transition: A practicum for baccalaureate nursing students. **Journal of Nursing Education, 21**(2), 32-37.
   c. Dear, M.R. and Keen, F. (1982). Promotion of self-care in the employee with rheumatoid arthritis. **Occupational Health Nursing, 30**(1), 32-34.

    d. Keen, F. (1979). Comparison of two intramuscular injection techniques. In B. L. Manger and K. Juggins (Eds.), **Vol. I: Abstracts of Nursing Research in the South.** Atlanta: Southern Regional Education Board.

    e. Keen, F. (1978). Comparison of two intermuscular injection techniques (Abstract). **Proceedings of the Arthritis Foundation Annual Scientific Meetings.** New York: The Arthritis Foundation.

4. Publication Under Editorial Review

    a. Keen, F. A model for relating nurse training to on-the-job performance. **Journal of Performance and Training.**

5. Research Reports

    a. Keen, F. (1983). Allied health workshop—final report. Illinois Department of Nursing. (ERIC Document Reproduction Service No. ED 000 000).

    b. Keen, F. and Ehlers, E. (1981). Health occupations cluster curriculum project, final report. Columbus: Southern University, Department of Nursing Education.

6. Course Materials

    a. Keen, F. (1984). **Learner's and instructor's guide to clinical procedures.** Unpublished manuscript.

    b. Keen, F. (1981). **Hazards of injection therapy.** Unpublished manuscript.

D. Papers/Presentations

1. Keen, F. (1984, August). Interdisciplinary and intercultural perspectives in professional education. Paper presented at the Second Multi-cultural and Interdisciplinary Development Education Conference with the University of the West Indies and Atlanta University, Kingston, Jamaica.

2. Keen, F. (1984, April). Comparison of two intramuscular injection techniques on the incidence and severity of discomfort and lesions at the injection site. Paper presented at the Clinical Research Day, University of Delaware.

3. Keen, F. (1982, March). An introduction to research methodology for nurses. Paper presented to the Excelsior Education Center Department of Nursing, Kingston, Jamaica.

4. Keen, F. (1980, December). Simplifying technical documents. Paper presented at the Sixth Annual Worskhop of Technical Writing, University of Northern Wisconsin.

VI. SERVICE ACTIVITIES

A. Service to the Institution

1. Department Service
   a. Chair, Graduate Affairs and Retention Committee, 1984-85.
   b. Member, Graduate Affairs and Retention Committee, 1983-84.
   c. Chair, Merit Pay Committee, 1981-82.
   d. Member, Curriculum Committee, 1981-83.
   e. Member, Program Reconciliation Sub-Committee, 1979-80.
   f. Member, Operating Paper Sub-Committee, 1978-79.
2. College Service
   a. Member, College of Applied Science Promotions Committee, 1983-84.
   b. Member, Dean's Search Committee, 1982-83.
   c. Member, ANA Report Committee, 1982-83.
   d. Member, Budget Advisory Committee, 1979-81.
3. University Service
   a. Chair, Intercollegiate Athletics Committee, 1983-84.
   b. Member, Intercollegiate Athletics Committee, 1982-83.
   c. Coordinator, Faculty Development Seminar, "Implementing a Faculty Promotion System", Summer, 1982.
   d. Member, Faculty Senate, 1980-83.
   e. Member, Foundation Fundraising Committee, 1979-81.

B. Professional Service

1. Professional Organizations
   a. American Association of Critical-Care Nurses
   b. American Association of University Professors
   c. American Public Health Association
   d. American Nurses Association
   e. Caribbean Nurses Organization
   f. National League for Nursing
   g. Council for International Health

2. Professional Appointments
   a. Chair, International Activities Sub-Committee of the American Association of Critical-Care Nurses, 1985-86.
   b. Member, International Activities Sub-Committee of the American Association of Critical-Care Nurses, 1982-86.
   c. Treasurer, Beta Tau Chapter, Sigma Theta Tau, National Honorary Society for Nursing, 1983.

     d. Reviewer, Medical-Surgical Nursing, **Nursing,** Springhouse Publishing Company, 1980 to present.

     e. Test Item Writer, Medical Nursing, National Council of State Boards of Nursing, National League for Nursing. September, 1979.

  3. Special Recognition

     a. Who's Who of American Women, 1984.

     b. Outstanding Young Women of America, 1982.

     c. Phi Kappa Phi, National Honors Society, 1975 to present.

     d. Sigma Theta Tau, National Honors Society of Nursing. 1975-1981.

  4. Consultantships

     a. Consulting Editor. Training Systems Designers, Carbondale, Illinois. Purpose: Consult on the content of a faculty development handbook. 1984-85.

     b. Technical Consultant. Cayman Hospital, Department of Nursing, Georgetown, Grand Cayman. Purpose: Development of in-service nursing education programs. August, 1984 to present.

     c. Curriculum Consultant. University of Miami School of Nursing, Coral Gables, Florida. Purpose: Revision of the graduate nursing curriculum. June, 1982.

     d. Technical Consultant. The John Hopkins School of Medicine, Department of Pharmacology and Experimental Therapeutics. Purpose: Design of clinical intramuscular drug study. May, 1981.

     e. Curriculum Consultant. Pan American Health Organization. Regional Office of the World Health Organization, Washington, D.C. Purpose: Development of curriculum and instructional materials for an intensive care nursing course at Princess Margaret Hospital, Bahamas. January, 1981.

C. Community Service

  1. Host, candidacy reception for State Senator William Robinson, October, 1985.

  2. Blood Pressure Screening Clinic with Regional Rotary Clubs, April, 1983.

  3. Illinois Heart Association, "Practical Aspects of Exercise Stress Testing". March, 1983.

  4. Comprehensive Health Planning, "Health Manpower Study". Spring, 1982.

  5. Commencement Address, "The Past, The Present and The Future". Associate Degree Nursing Program, Black Diamond Community

College. May, 1981.

6. Metro High School, Careers Day, "Medical and Allied Health Occupations". September, 1980.

7. Memorial Hospital, "Rewriting Job Descriptions of Critical-Care Nurses". October, 1979.

D. Administration

1. Department

a. Program Coordinator, Off-campus Nursing Education program, Harrison, Illinois, 1984 to present.

b. Graduate Program Coordinator, 1980-84.

c. Undergraduate Program Coordinator, 1979-81.

d. Coordinator, Hospital Internship Program, 1978-80.

2. College

a. Assistant to the Dean, Summer, 1982.
b. Foreign Student Advisor, 1981-82.

3. University

a. University Administrative Intern, Academic Year, 1977-78.

E. Professional Development

1. Mini-sabbatical. Cook County General Hospital, Critical-Care Nursing Unit. Interim, Summer-Fall, 1986.

2. Critical-Care Nursing Workshop, San Francisco, California, 1983.

3. Rheumatoid Arthritis Workshop, 1981.

4. National League for Nursing conventions, 1974 to present.

VII. PROFESSIONAL PRACTICE ACTIVITIES

A. Clinical Practice

1. Critical-Care Nursing. Memorial Hospital, Columbus, Illinois. Summers, 1982 to present.

2. Emergency Medical Care Team. Southern University Health Services, 1979-83.

B. Administrative Practice

1. Assistant to the Director of Nurses, Interim, Fall-Spring Semesters, 1982-84.

CHAPTER 8

Promotion Dossier

The promotion dossier is the document that represents the faculty member in the academic tenure and/or promotion process. The dossier is a record of the teaching, research, service and professional practice activities of the faculty member from time of initial employment or last promotion to the present. (See Example F.)

The promotion dossier is prepared by the faculty member and submitted to the chairperson in accordance with the institution's promotion policy. Depending on the policies of the department, college and institution, the dossier may or may not be accompanied by the materials that resulted from the faculty member's professional activity and involvement. (See Chapter Five.)

Organization

A title page and table of contents introduces the promotion dossier. The title page contains the title of the document, i.e. "Promotion Dossier", name and current rank of the faculty member, date of submission and names of the parent department, college and institution. The table of contents lists the entries presented in the document and the pages on which they appear.

The first section of the dossier provides a brief history of the candidate. It includes the date of employment of the faculty member, academic title at time of employment, highest degree earned, degree required, special qualifications, past professional experience, changes following employment at the parent institution, and nature of the assignment since initial employment or last promotion.

The body of the promotion dossier reflects the organizational structure initially established in the department plan and repeated in each succeeding document of the faculty recognition system. However, unlike any of the preceding components of the system, the purpose of the dossier is to document the teaching, research, service and professional practice activities of the faculty member for purposes of academic promotion and/or awarding of tenure.

The last section of the dossier contains the faculty member's letter confirming his/her desire to enter the promotion process and letters from the chairperson of the department and dean of the college or school recommending or not endorsing the candidate's promotion. (See Appendices A, B and C in Example F.) The recommendation of the chairperson and dean accompany the dossier to central administration where the chief academic administrator of the institution concurs with or does not support the positions of the chairperson and dean.

Content

The four major sections of the promotion dossier are Documentation of Teaching and Related Activities, Documentation of Research and Scholarly Activities, Documentation of Service Activities and Documentation of Professional Practice Activities.

Documentation of Teaching and Related Activities

The Documentation of Teaching and Related Activities section of the promotion dossier includes student evaluations, peer evaluations and other types of support of the faculty member's teaching effort.

Student Evaluations: Two types of student evaluations are shown in Example F. The first is a quantitative summary of the faculty member's classroom performance. The second is a list of qualitative statements from students regarding the faculty member's teaching. Solicited letters of support from students are also included in the student evaluation section.

Peer Evaluations: Peer evaluations are letters solicited by the chairperson from faculty members and colleagues who know the teaching abilities of the faculty member. Most letters include the length of time the author has known the candidate professionally, examples demonstrating the basis of support and a definitive statement recommending the faculty member for promotion.

Depending on the promotion policies of the department, college and institution, the faculty member may be expected to provide a list of peers to the chairperson for solicitation or the chair would assume the responsibility of selecting individuals for recommendation. In many cases, a combination of the two approaches occurs.

Other Support: Unsolicited letters and other types of written comment comprise this portion of the documentation section. Entries may be from students, parents or colleagues who know the candidate's ability to work with students in and out of the classroom.

Documentation of Research and Scholarly Activities

The Documentation of Research and Scholarly Activities section includes funded research, scholarly activities, peer evaluations and other support.

Funded Research: The funded research portion of the section lists the research grants and projects awarded to the candidate, the agencies underwriting the grants/projects, and the dollar amount of the award per grant/project.

Scholarly Activities: The scholarly activities portion of the research section of the promotion dossier contains a listing of the various publications and presentations of the faculty member. The list includes the books, chapters, journal articles, etc. and papers and presentations made by the faculty member.

Accompanying each entry in the list is an evaluation by the chairperson. In Example F, the evaluation includes a quantitative score (selected from a predetermined scale) with a narrative description of the activity.

Other types of creative activity are also reported in the scholarly activities portion of the dossier. In addition to publishing and making formal presentations, a faculty member who is involved in the fine arts, music, theater, etc. also reports his/her creative and artistic works here. Appropriate headings are used to distinguish the different activities.

Peer Evaluations: Much like the peer evaluation portion of the teaching documentation section, peer evaluations of the faculty member's research and scholarly activity most often are in the form of letters solicited by and directed to the department chairperson. The letters address the issues of continued research contribution, timeliness, relevancy of topics, originality and precision of thought. The letters are concluded with a recommendation for promotion of the faculty member.

Other Support: "Other Support", as it pertains to research and scholarly activity, includes unsolicited letters and written comments regarding the faculty member's research, publications, presentations and/or other creative work. In most cases, the unsolicited letters are addressed to the faculty member recognizing his/her scholarly contributions.

Documentation of Service Activities

The third major section in the promotion dossier concerns the documentation of service activities. The section lists the faculty member's service contributions to the institution, profession and community. It also itemizes the administrative assignments and professional development activities of the faculty member.

Service to the Institution: Service to the institution is categorized into department, college and university service. The activities included under each heading denote the individual and group service activities in which the faculty member has been involved. Letters solicited by the chairperson document the faculty member's service activities.

Professional Service: The professional service portion of the promotion dossier includes the list of professional organizations to which the faculty member belongs, appointments to professional organizations and committees, recognition for special accomplishments and consultantships to groups requiring the candidate's special expertise. Letters of support solicited by the chairperson accompany the list of service contributions of the faculty member to the profession.

Community Service: The list of contributions of the faculty member as a representative of the department, college and/or institution to individuals and groups in the community comprises the community contribution of the local, state, national and international levels.

Letters solicited by the chairperson supporting the faculty member's involvement and contribution accompany the list of community service items.

Administration: As discussed earlier in the handbook, the administrative activities of a faculty member are viewed as service contributions to the department, college or institution. Typical administrative assignments held by faculty members include directorships, coordinatorships and advisory positions. The entries in the administrative portion of the dossier include the title of the position, name of the group or organization being served and dates of the assignment.

Letters of support addressed to the chairperson accompany the list of assignments.

Professional Development: Professional development encompasses those activities performed by the faculty member to keep abreast of new ideas and changes in the discipline or profession. As shown in Example F, types of professional development include such activities as sabbaticals and attendance at conventions, professional meetings, seminars and workshops. Any activity specifically designed to enhance professional growth qualifies as professional development.

Documentation of the faculty member's participation in the professional development activities accompanies the list of items.

Documentation of Professional Practice Activities

The categorization and listing of professional practice activities is dictated by the particular situation of the faculty member. In Example F, the two types of activities reported are "Clinical Practice" and "Administrative Practice." The entries under each heading define the type of activity, where it occurred and the dates of its occurrence.

Reflecting the organization, content and style of the curriculum vitae, the activities listed in the professional practice section of the promotion dossier, as well as those listed in the teaching, research and service sections, are arranged in descending chronological order with the most recent entries heading the lists.

Curriculum Vitae

A current curriculum vitae is included in the promotion dossier. The vitae supplements the dossier with a comprehensive profile of the candidate.

Example F

Promotion Dossier

for

Dr. Frances Keen

Associate Professor

September, 1986

Department of Nursing Education

College of Applied Science

Southern University

85

Table of Contents

I. HISTORY OF THE CANDIDATE

   A. Date of employment: July 1, 1976

   B. Title at time of employment: Assistant Professor

   C. Highest degree earned: Doctor of Nursing Science

   D. Degree required: Doctor of Nursing Science

   E. Special Qualifications:

      1. Hospital nursing experience.

      2. Hospital or school-based teaching experience.

      3. Experience in program development.

   F. Professional Experience:

      1. Assistant Professor, University of Maryland School of Nursing, Graduate Faculty, Medical-Surgical Nursing, Baltimore, Maryland. August 1974-June 1976.

      2. Clinical Nurse, Medical-Surgical Float Pool, The John Hopkins Hospital, Baltimore, Maryland. January 1975-June 1976.

      3. Nursing Curriculum Researcher, The John Hopkins University School of Hygiene and Public Health, Baltimore, Maryland. July 1974-March 1975.

      4. Visiting Nurse, Extended Service Unit, Visiting Nurse Association, Baltimore, Maryland. Summer 1974.

      5. Instructor, The John Hopkins University School of Health Services, Nursing Education Program, Baltimore, Maryland. February 1971-July 1974.

   G. Changes Following Employment

      1. Degrees Attained: None

      2. Promotions Earned: From Assistant Professor to Associate Professor with tenure. Date: April 1982.

      3. Other Professional Achievements:
        a. Appointment to the Graduate Faculty, Fall 1980.

   H. Nature of Assignment Since Promotion

      1. Direct teaching in undergraduate and graduate on-campus and off-campus courses in the department

      2. Securing of and work on funded projects

      3. Professional writing

      4. Coordination of special programs

      5. University, professional and community service

SECTION II

DOCUMENTATION OF TEACHING AND
RELATED ACTIVITIES

- A. Student Evaluations
  B. Peer Evaluations
  C. Other Support

INSTRUCTOR AND COURSE EVALUATION

Course: NE 460 - Adult Health Nursing II

Location: Campus

Date: Spring 1984

I. Personal/Interpersonal

Knew if students understood her/him	8
Spoke understandably	9
Answered impromptu questions satisfactorily	8
Showed an interest in the course	8
Accepted criticism and suggestions	6
Showed an interest in students	8
Was available outside of class	9
Encouraged student participation	8

II. Course Structuring by Instruction

Prepared for class	9
Made clear assignments	6
Set clear standards for grading	2
Graded fairly	8
Gave several examples to explain complex ideas	8
Increased appreciation for the subject	8
Organized and presesnted subject matter well	9
Specified objectives of the course	9
Achieved the specified objectives of the course	9
Explained the subject clearly	9
Was enthusiastic about the subject	8
The course was well organized	8
The tests covered the course material well	9
Audio-visuals could be used more effectively	9
In general, taught the class effectively	8

III. Course Quality

This course was a good learning experience	8
The content of this course was good	8
I had trouble paying attention in class	7
This course was very interesting	8
This course was one of the best I have taken	8
This course was a waste of time	1
The textbook was good	9
This course should be taught in some other way	8
I covered this material in other courses	7
This course should continue to be offered	8
Generally, the course was good	8

Note: Evaluation scale: 1 low - 9 high.

92

Written Comments from Students

The following comments are taken from the written responses section of the computer form. They are the students' responses to the question "What is your overall opinion of the instructor?".

"Excellent. Knows material well and was able to present it clearly and concisely". Spring, 1982.

"The instructor was well organized and sincerely interested in her work". Spring, 1982.

"She is very knowledgeable and enthusiastic about the material she's teaching". Spring, 1982.

" . . . a very colorful and informative person (easy to learn from and sensitive to her students' thoughts and ideas)". Spring, 1982.

"Extremely well prepared and seems to enjoy her field. Made the course definitely well worth taking". Fall, 1981.

"Very knowledgeable and enthusiastic about subject". Fall, 1981.

"Well organized, efficient, and highly motivated individual". Spring, 1981.

"The instructor was very good, she enjoyed teaching the course and believed in what she was teaching". Spring, 1981.

"Very well organized—very "student" oriented. Excellent instructor - available to students". Spring, 1980.

"Dr. Keen seems to have a **strong** interest in this subject. I feel she taught this course in about the most interesting way possible. She's highly organized which makes for easy understanding". Spring, 1980.

"Truly enjoyed her approach to teaching—keeps students interested". Summer, 1980.

"Dr. Keen is a very enthusiastic instructor and its projected over to the student so very well until the student gains more enthusiasm. She is always available to assist students". Spring, 1979.

"The instructor was excellent. I feel that she is one of the best instructors that we have had". Spring, 1979.

"Dr. Keen was truly a model instructor with a professional attitude. She treated each student as an individual and with respect. I certainly hope we might have her as our instructor again". Fall, 1979.

SECTION II

DOCUMENTATION OF TEACHING AND RELATED.ACTIVITIES

A. Student Evaluations
• B. Peer Evaluations
C. Other Support

September 20, 1986

Dr. Catherine Roberts, Chair
Department of Nursing Education
College of Applied Science
Southern University
Columbia, IL 62888

Dear Dr. Roberts:

I have been asked by Frances Keen to comment on her teaching
effectiveness in consideration for promotion to Professor. I've known
Fran for more than 12 years and believe my observations are valid.

As a new faculty member in 1977, I was pleased to be welcomed by
Fran and to receive her offer of assistance. She willingly shared
various course outlines and related resource materials and visuals. I
was impressed to discover the level of detail that she follows in
preparing instructional materials. Fran is a meticulous planner and
organizer. The quality of her instructional materials are more akin to
final manuscript copy than to teaching materials. As a matter of fact,
her course materials have evolved into a commercial text and numerous
articles and presentations.

Fran is intellectually honest and a defender of academic principles
and freedom. She subscribes to high academic standards and has the
courage to judge student work in relation to its true merit. I've
worked with her on numerous graduate committees and have always found
her to be cooperative and conscientious. Fran is highly motivated and
interested in her teaching and work with students.

Although I've never observed Fran teaching in an actual classroom
situation, I have observed her "teaching" in many other environments.
She is self confident and has a relaxed, informal teaching style. I
anticipate that her friendliness and good sense of humor are reflected in
her classroom teaching.

Dr. Keen is an established, knowledgable, veteran teacher in
the field of nursing. In my opinion, she surpasses all the stated
criteria for promotion in rank. I am proud to have her as a friend
and colleague. I recommend her for promotion to Professor without
reservation or qualification.

Sincerely,

Larry Bailey
Professor

LJB:JTF

SECTION II

DOCUMENTATION OF TEACHING AND RELATED ACTIVITIES

A. Student Evaluations
B. Peer Evaluations
- C. Other Support

April 17, 1983

Dr. Frances Keen
Department of Nursing Education
Southern University
Columbia, IL   62888

Dear Dr. Keen,

I would like to take the opportunity to tell you how much I appreciated your help in this past year. There is no question that your courses in Adult Health Care Nursing were the finest, most beneficial courses I have yet taken on a college campus. You not only know your subject matter extremely well, but have the ability to organize and present the information so your students can understand it. I appreciate the time and effort you put into the class.

Take care of yourself and keep on running during those lunch periods! Thanks for all your help.

Your grateful student,

Carolyn Lawson

Carolyn Lawson

SECTION III.

DOCUMENTATION OF RESEARCH AND SCHOLARLY ACTIVITIES

- A. Funded Research
- B. Scholarly Activities
- C. Peer Evaluations
- D. Other Support

A. Funded Research

Principal Investigator	Title and Purpose of Project	Funding Agency	Funding
F. Keen	"A Study to Examine the Relationships Between Self-Concept and Health-Seeking Behaviors". Purpose: To determine if there is a similarity in self-concept in people who seek health care. January 1, 1986 - June 30, 1987.	National Institutes of Health	$46,000
F. Keen	"Competency-Based Nursing Education Project". Purpose: To develop a competency-based nursing program. October 1, 1984 - September 30, 1986.	Illinois Department of Nursing	$42,000
F. Keen and J. Fisher	"Peace Corps Recruiting Grant". Purpose: To identify nursing personnel to serve in the Peace Corps. July 1, 1984 - June 30, 1985.	ACTION/Peace Corps	$15,000
F. Keen and F. Raisen	"Development of a Model Curriculum for a Master's Degree Level Outreach Nursing Program". Purpose: To develop an exemplary nursing program in Illinois and surrounding states. September 1, 1983 - August 30, 1984.	National Association of Practicing	$82,000

SECTION III

DOCUMENTATION OF RESEARCH AND
SCHOLARLY ACTIVITIES

A.   Funded Research
- B.   Scholarly Activities
C.   Peer Evaluations
D.   Other Support

B.   Scholarly Activities

Evaluate the following contributions of the faculty members in terms of their contribution to the field and the reputation of the organization publishing the material. If a creative activity, evaluate the originality of the work and its contribution to the field. Use the following scale in evaluating each item.

5 - Outstanding contribution, highly prestigious, peer evaluated
4 - Significant contribution, much respected, peer evaluated
3 - Worthy contribution, selective
2 - Of value, serves wide range of contribution
1 - Low quality, not discriminating
0 - Not acceptable
X - No basis for judgment

1.   Publications: Chairperon's Evaluation

   a.   Books

     1)   Keen, F. (1985). **Rheumatic di-**   (5)Contribution to
        sease nursing—a primer.   professional area
        Carbondale: Training Sys-   of interest.
        tems Designers.

     2)   Keen, F. and Dunbar, S. (1983).   (4)Contribution to
        A suggested program of   professional area
        study for preparing health-   of interest.
        care aides. Atlanta: Gray
        Press.

   b.   Chapters in Professional Books

     1)   Keen, F. (1983). Nursing as a   (5)Contribution to
        profession. In W. Leka,   professional area
        Career guide to medical and   of interest.
        health care occupations.
        Carbondale: Training Sys-
        tems Designers.

   c.   Articles in Professional Journals

     1)   Keen, F. (1985). Development of   (5)Refereed journal.
        extension programs to meet
        community needs. **Journal**
        of Nursing Education,
        29(1), 39-41.

     2)   Dear, M. R. and Keen, F. (1983).   (4)Professional Journal.
        Role transition: A practi-
        cum   for   baccalaureate
        nursing students. **Journal of**
        Nursing Education, 21(2),
        32-37.

     3)   Dear, M.R. and Keen, F. (1982).   (4)Refereed journal.
        Promotion of self-care in

the employee with rheu-
matoid arthritis. **Occupational Health Nursing,
30**(1), 32-34.

d.   Publication Under Editorial Review
1)   Keen, F. A model for relating   (5)Refereed journal.
nurse training to on-the-job
performance. **Journal of
Performance and Training.**

e.   Research Reports
1)   Keen, F. (1983). Allied health   (5)Report of findings
workshop—final report.   of research project.
Illinois   Department
of Nursing. (ERIC Docu-
ment Reproduction Service
No. ED 000 000).

f.   Course Materials
1)   Keen, F. (1984). **Learner's and   (5)Product of curriculum
instructor's guide to clinical**   development work in
procedures. Unpublished   professionial area.
manuscript.

2.   Papers/Presentations
a.   Keen, F. (1984, August). Interdis-   (4)Paper presented at the
ciplinary and intercultural   invitation of the two
perspectives in professioinal   host schools.
education. Paper presented
at   the   Second   Multi-
cultural   and   Interdisciplinary Development Educa-
tion Conference with the
University of the West Indies and Atlanta University, Kingston, Jamaica.

b.   Keen, F. (1984, April). Compari-   (5)Paper presented at the
son of two intramuscular   invitation of the host
injection techniques on the   institution.
incidence and severity of
discomfort and lesions at
the injection site. Paper
presented at the Clinical
Research Day, University
of Delaware.

c.   Keen, F. (1982, March). An intro-   (5)Paper presented at
duction to research meth-   annual meeting of
odology for nurses. Paper   Jamaican nurses.
presented to the Excelsior
Education Center Depart-
ment of Nursing, Kingston,
Jamaica.

SECTION III

DOCUMENTATION OF RESEARCH AND SCHOLARLY ACTIVITIES

A. Funded Research
B. Scholarly Activities
- C. Peer Evaluations
D. Other Support

September 29, 1986

Dr. Catherine Roberts, Chair
Department of Nursing Education
College of Applied Science
Southern University
Columbus, IL 62888

Dear Dr. Roberts:

I am more than happy to respond to the questions raised in your letter about the professional performance of Dr. Frances Keen and her research and scholarly activities. If, after reading my comments, you have any further questions, please call me.

My professional relationship with Dr. Keen began in 1977 when I was serving as the Health Occupations Editor for Technical Publications, Inc. I contracted Dr. Keen's services as a content/methodology special- ist for the purpose of assisting me in the development of educational materials (i.e. books, study guides, video supplements, etc.) in nursing education. I selected Dr. Keen over other candidates for the position for the following reasons:

1) Dr. Keen had a demonstrated commitment to the improvement of teaching technique and educational materials in nursing education. Her original research, student generated work and the educational materials she had personally authored convinced me of this commitment.

2) After checking with Dr. Keen's references, I was assured that she could meet the company's demands of consultants and could meet the often critical deadlines required in publishing.

3) A review of her original research in nursing education by practitioners brought praise for originality and pre- cision of thought.

4) Personal meetings with Dr. Keen convinced me that she had the ability to pursue cooperative endeavors with enthus- iasm and a degree of conviviality too often lacking in others I had interviewed.

Dr. Keen and I continued working together until I left Technical Publications in May, 1979. During that time we had an excellent working relationship. Her direct involvement in the development of educational materials was considerable. Conservatively, I would say that her efforts -- subsumed between the covers of books written by others -- influenced approximately 50,000 students.

In closing, I would like to add that in my 12 years experience in academic publishing and having worked with a variety of different types of consultants, Dr. Keen ranks in the top 1%.

Regards,

Preston Mathews, President
Wayne County Press

SECTION III

DOCUMENTATION OF RESEARCH AND SCHOLARLY ACTIVITIES

A. Funded Research
B. Scholarly Activities
C. Peer Evaluations
• D. Other Support

September 29, 1979
RE: Manuscript #96

Dear Dr. Keen:

Your manuscript, "Comparison of Two Intramuscular Injection Techniques" will be published in Volume I - Abstracts of Nursing Research in the South. That issue of the Abstracts will be mailed by the printer approximately December 1, 1979.

Your manuscript will be considered for an Outstanding Manuscript Award. The description of the award categories and review process are contained on page 62 of Volume 19, Number 2 issue of the Abstracts. For purposes of that competition, your manuscript has been classified as "Research". Please review the criteria for that category and inform me if this classification is correct.

Again, congratulations on having your manuscript accepted for publication. Abstracts of Nursing Research in the South is one of the premier referred publications in the nation. The editorial board is always interested in reviewing quality manuscripts for possible publication. We hope you will consider submitting future work to the Southern Regional Education Board.

Sincerely,

George S. Skalsky
Editor

SECTION IV

DOCUMENTATION OF SERVICE
ACTIVITIES

- A. Service to the Institution
        Department
        College
        University
  B. Professional Service
  C. Community Service
  D. Administration
  E. Professional Development

A.   Service to the Institution

1.   Department Service
- a. Chair, Graduate Affairs and Retention Committee, 1984-85.
- b. Member, Graduate Affairs and Retention Committee, 1983-84.
- c. Chair, Merit Pay Committee, 1981-82.

2.   College Service
- a. Member, College of Applied Science Promotions Committee, 1983-84.
- b. Member, Dean's Search Committee, 1982-83.
- c. Member, ANA Report Committee, 1982-83.

3.   University Service
- a. Chair, Intercollegiate Athletics Committee, 1983-84.
- b. Member, Intercollegiate Athletics Committee, 1982-83.
- c. Coordinator, Faculty Development Seminar, "Implementing a Faculty Promotion System", Summer, 1982.
- d. Member, Faculty Senate, 1980-83.

September 30, 1986

Dr. Catherine Roberts, Chair
Department of Nursing Education
College of Applied Science
Southern University
Columbia, IL 62888

Dear Dr. Roberts:

I am pleased to comply with your request to write a letter for the purpose of evaluating Dr. Frances Keen's service contributions. I do not believe many faculty in the Department, College, or University are more seriously dedicated than Dr. Keen to providing and maintaining a strong professional image of the University and its many programs.

This dedication and conscientious effort is reflected in a variety of service activities. At the international level she has been responsible for an on-going Peace Corps effort since 1978. In addition, she has consulted with the Pan American Health Organization regarding the preparation of nurses and allied health personnel. She has also been involved with projects in Yugoslavia, New Zealand, and Australia.

Dr. Keen has provided assistance to secondary, post-secondary, and community groups throughout the state of Illinois in such areas as directing workshops, curriculum design, community surveys, feasibility studies, and educational program development.

During the spring and summer semesters of 1981, Dr. Keen provided a most valuable service to the Department by working with the faculty to develop and standardize course outcomes and improve course offerings in general.

Dr. Keen has consistently been involved in a variety of University, College, and Departmental committee activities. In every instance, she has approached her responsibilities energetically and enthusiastically.

Consultantships and contacts with individuals in various national and state agencies have resulted in a sharing of ideas with faculty and students via the Nursing Department's Summer Seminar series. These have included publishers, agency directors, and persons of high repute in many facets of Nursing Education.

I believe Dr. Keen's service contributions have been valuable to many people directly and indirectly associated with education. I wish her success in her request for promotion.

Sincerely,

Jeanne Fisher

Jeanne Fisher

JF

SECTION IV

DOCUMENTATION OF SERVICE
ACTIVITIES

A. Service to the Institution
   Department
   College
   University
• B. Professional Service
  C. Community Service
  D. Administration
  E. Professional Development

B. Professional Service

1. Memberships in Professional Organizations
    a. American Association of Critical-Care Nurses
    b. American Association of University Professors
    c. American Public Health Association
    d. American Nurses Association
    e. Caribbean Nurses Organization
    f. National League of Nursing
    g. Council for International Health

2. Professional Appointments
    a. Chair, International Activities Sub-Committee of the American Association of Critical-Care Nurses, 1985-86.
    b. Member, International Activities Sub-Committee of the American Association of Critical-Care Nurses, 1982-86.
    c. Treasurer, Beta Tau Chapter, Sigma Theta Tau, National Honorary Society for Nursing, 1983.
    d. Reviewer, Medical-Surgical Nursing, **Nursing**, Springhouse Publishing Company, 1980 to present.

3. Special Recognition
    a. Who's Who of American Women, 1984.
    b. Outstanding Young Women of America, 1982.
    c. Phi Kappa Phi, National Honors Society of Nursing, 1975 to present.

4. Consultantships
    a. Consulting Editor. Training Systems Designers, Carbondale, Illinois. Purpose: Consult on the content of a faculty development handbook. 1984-85.
    b. Technical Consultant. Cayman Hospital, Department of Nursing, Georgetown, Grand Cayman. Purpose: Development of in-service nursing education programs. August, 1984 to present.
    c. Curriculum Consultant. University of Miami School of Nursing, Coral Gables, Florida. Purpose: Revision of the graduate nursing curriculum. June, 1982.

October 19, 1986

Dr. Catherine Roberts, Chair
Department of Nursing Education
College of Applied Science
Southern University
Columbia, IL 62888

Dear Dr. Roberts:

The following information is presented in support of Dr. Frances
Keen's promotion to Professor.

For approximately two years Dr. Keen has served as a member of the
Association of Institutions of Research National Review Panel. During
that time, she has been an active and contributing member of the panel.
She serves the group and its constituencies well by being an articulate
and strong proponent of institutional research and by providing "leadership through example" via her own professional research endeavors.

Active membership on the Review Panel takes time, energy and
commitment. Dr. Keen has willingly given of each in supporting the
goals of the Panel and extending the bounds of institutional research.
Her contributions to the profession in the area of research will prove
invaluable over time.

Thank you for the opportunity to support Dr. Keen's promotion.

As always,

Respectfully yours,

Howard E. Hesketh

Howard Hesketh
Director
Association of Institutions
  of Research

HH:EE

SECTION IV

DOCUMENTATION OF SERVICE ACTIVITIES

A. Service to the Institution

   Department
   College
   University
B. Professional Service
• C. Community Service
D. Administration
E. Professional Development

C.   Community Service

1.   Host. Candidacy reception for State Senator William Robinson, October, 1985.

2.   Blood Pressure Screening Clinic with regional Rotary Clubs, April, 1983.

3.   Illinois Heart Association, "Practical Aspects of Exercise Stress Testing". March, 1983.

4.   Comprehensive Health Planning, "Health Manpower Study". Spring, 1982.

October 29, 1986

Professor Catherine Roberts
Chairperson
Department of Nursing Education
Southern University
Columbia, IL 62888

Dear Professor Roberts:

Judy, my wife, and I had the unique opportunity of meeting a
number of friends at a reception hosted for us by Frances Keen.
The purpose of the reception was to rally support for my candidacy
of state senator of Illinois.

Fran, in an effort to better educate some of their friends on
the practical side of politics, as well as give them opportunity to
meet a "living politico", invited about 100 people to the reception
at her apartment. As we all hoped, the party was a tremendous success.
About 80 people who received invitations came and another 30-35 dropped
by when they heard about the reception.

My compliments to you on having on your faculty a person who is
interested in both the university and the community. Please express
my heartfelt thanks to Fran for all of her effort.

Respectfully yours,

Bill

William Robinson
State Senator

WR:JF

SECTION IV

DOCUMENTATION OF SERVICE ACTIVITIES

A. Service to the Institution

    Department
    College
    University
B. Professional Service
C. Community Service
- D. Administration
E. Professional Development

D. Administration

1. Department
    a. Program Coordinator, Off-campus Nursing Education program, Harrison, Illinois, 1984 to present.
    b. Graduate Program Coordinator, 1980-84.

2. College
    a. Assistant to the Dean, summer, 1982.
    b. Foreign Student Advisor, 1981-82.

3. University
    a. None

August 17, 1982

Dr. Frances Keen
Department of Nursing Education
Southern University
Columbus, IL   62888

Dear Fran:

I want to thank you for your participation in the graduation
program at Springfield. From all reports, your commencement
address was a resounding success.

As we discussed when you first joined us, a faculty member's
job takes you down many roads. The keynote speaker assignment
was just one of these. Congratulations on your success. May it
be the first of many.

Respectfully yours,

Theodore Bulla, Dean
College of Applied Science

SECTION IV

DOCUMENTATION OF SERVICE
ACTIVITIES

A. Service to the Institution

    Department
    College
    University
B. Professional Service
C. Community Service
D. Administration
- E. Professional Development

E.   Professional Development

1.   Mini-sabbatical. Cook County General Hospital, Critical-Care Nursing Unit. Interim, summer-fall, 1986.

2.   National League for Nursing conventions, 1974 to present.

3.   Critical-Care Nursing Workshop, San Francisco, California, 1983.

SECTION V

DOCUMENTATION OF PROFESSIONAL
PRACTICE ACTIVITIES

- Clinical Practice
  Administrative Practice

A. Clinical Practice

1. Critical-Care Nursing. Memorial Hospital, Columbus, Illinois. Summers, 1982 to present.
2. Emergency Medical Care Team. Southern University Health Services. 1979-83.

SECTION V

DOCUMENTATION OF PROFESSIONAL PRACTICE ACTIVITIES

Clinical Practice
• Administrative Practice

B.   Administrative Practice

1.   Assistant to the Director of Nurses. Interim, Fall-Spring semesters, 1982-84.

VII. APPENDIX

Faculty Member's Letter of

Confirmation

September 11, 1986

Dr. Catherine Roberts, Chairperson
Department of Nursing Education
Southern University

Dear Dr. Roberts:

     This letter certifies that I have reviewed my dossier
and that the entries and substantiation thereof are accurate.

                         Respectfully yours,

                         Frances Keen
                         Associate Professor
                         Nursing Education

FK:SJ

Chairperson's Letter of Recommendation

November 15, 1986

Dr. Theodore Buila, Dean
College of Applied Science
Southern University

Dear Dean Buila:

    This letter is to recommend the promotion of Dr. Frances
Keen to Professor. She received unanimous support from the
11 full professors in this department. All agreed that
her teaching, research, service and professional practice
contributions since her promotion to Associate Professor
has been of exceptional quality. I agree.

    It is with great pleasure that we recommend her to you.

                        Sincerely yours,

                        Catherine Roberts
                        Chair
                        Nursing Education

CR:jrw

Dean's Letter of Recommendation

December 21, 1986

Dr. Albert Somit, Vice President
Academic Studies
Southern University

Dear Dr. Somit:

I am forwarding to you the promotion dossier for Dr. Frances
Keen. Dr. Keen has been recommended for promotion to the rank
of Professor by a vote of 11-0 in the Department of Nursing
Education. The College of Applied Science Promotion Committee
concurred and voted 7 in favor, 1 opposed for promotion.

Dr. Keen has established an enviable reputation in the
classroom. She is viewed as being a demanding, but fair, teacher.
Here peers view her as exceptionally strong in course organization
and in providing quality experiences for her students.

Dr. Keen has continued her excellent publishing record over
the years. Since 1982 (time of her promotion to Associate
Professor), she has completed a nursing text, co-authored a
curriculum guide in the health field, and authored a chapter in
a professional book. She has also authored a number of articles
in referred journals. Her record of papers presented nationally
and internationally is equally impressive.

Frances is active in her service activities to the University,
profession and community. Currently, she is serving as a consulting
editor to Training Systems Designers and as a technical nursing
consultant in the Caribbean.

I recommend to you that Dr. Frances Keen be promoted to the
rank of Professor in the Department of Nursing Education.

With respect,

Theodore Buila, Dean
College of Applied Science

TB:jrw

EVALUATION AND IMPLEMENTATION

CHAPTER 9

Evaluating Faculty Performance

For the faculty recognition system to be complete, a fair and equitable plan for evaluating the academic activities and contributions of the faculty is needed. Documentation and evaluation of teaching, research, service and professional practice is the basis for recognizing and rewarding faculty performance. Success in each area of activity justifies annual salary increase and merit pay. Also, success in the respective areas establishes a balance of teaching, research, service and professional practice activity that leads to the eventual awarding of tenure and academic promotion.

Documentation

In review, documentation of the faculty member's teaching, research, service and professional practice activities begins with the preparation of an annual plan of activities. Reflecting the organization and intent of the department plan, the annual plan is a proposal of what the faculty member intends to do in the ensuing academic or calendar year. The annual plan is put into operation by the department chairperson by way of semester or quarterly assignments given to the faculty member. As the year passes, the faculty member keeps record of his/her accomplishments in the activities card file and samples file.

The faculty member reports his/her accomplishments at the end of the academic or calendar year in the annual achievement report. The organization and content of the report parallel those of the annual plan. Comparison of the two documents reveals the degree of success of the faculty member in attaining the stated objectives.

The achievements of the faculty member, as stated in the achievement report, are then entered in the curriculum vitae and promotion dossier. The vitae and dossier respectively serve as a permanent record of professional activity and support the faculty member in the academic promotion process.

Evaluation

Evaluation, as it applies to the faculty recognition system, serves a dual purpose. First, performance of the faculty member is evaluated for the immediate need of determining salary increase and merit pay. Second, the evaluation process is used with longer term implications to determine the awarding of tenure and academic promotion.

Salary and Merit Pay

A comparison of the faculty member's annual plan and achievement report provides the basis for determining salary increase and merit pay. The comparison also shows the degree of success realized by the faculty member in attaining the stated objectives. See Figure 9.1.

Annual Plan	Achievement Report
Research	**Research**
Objective #1—Seek funding to examine relationships between self-concept and health-seeking behaviors.	**Objective #1**—Seek funding to examine relationships between self-concept and health-seeking behaviors.
Completion Date: June 30, 1987	**Completion Date:** June 30, 1987
Resources: Secretarial help, graduate assistance	**Progress:** Project funded. Developed and pilot-tested written test instruments

Figure 9.1 - Comparison of Entries in
the Annual Plan and Achievement Report

If the faculty member adds objectives to the annual plan, substitutes entries during the year, or deletes selected items, the changes are reflected in the achievement report. Comparisons would be made between the updated version of the annual plan and the achievement report.

Scoring

Several approaches are available to determine the success of the faculty member in attaining the stated objectives. One approach is to qualitatively evaluate the faculty member's performance. See Figure 9.2.

Research

Objective #1—Seek funding to examine relationships between self-concept and health-seeking behaviors.

☐ Exceeded expectations

☐ Attained objective

☐ Some progress toward objective

☐ No progress toward objective

Figure 9.2 - Qualitative Evaluation

As the objectives in each major section of the annual plan and achievement report are compared, the faculty member's performance is determined according to one of the four criteria. Attainment of the objective is the accepted standard. Also, exceptional performance is recognized together with the acknowledgement of some or no progress being made toward the objective.

If desired, the above approach can be quantified. A numerical value can be assigned to each criteria statement. In the numerical form, totals can be computed and average scores determined which are then used in the evaluation process.

Another approach is to assign points to each type of teaching, research, service and professional practice activity. For example, a research proposal might be valued by the department faculty as 10 points; a funded research grant, 30 points; a refereed journal article, 25 points; a non-refereed journal article, 10 points; a course taught, 25 points; and so on. With a point system in place, the total numerical value of the objectives attained and reported in the achievement report can be compared to the total number of points possible in the annual plan. A measure of the achievement of the faculty member can be determined from the comparison. See Figure 9.3.

$$\frac{\text{Annual Achievement Report}}{\text{Annual Plan of Activities}}$$

$$= \frac{\text{Actual points earned}}{\text{Total points possible}} \times 100$$

$$= \% \text{ of total points possible}$$

Example

$$\frac{424}{482} \times 100 = 87.9\%$$

Scale

%	Rating
85 - 100	Excellent
55 - 84	Acceptable
0 - 54	Needs Improvement

Figure 9.3 - Quantitative Comparison of the
Annual Plan and Achievement Report

In the above figure, the points have been converted to percentages to simplify the rating process. By using percentages, faculty members can tailor their annual plans to their interests and abilities and, yet, be evaluated on a uniform standard in the department. The range of percentage points for "Excellent", "Acceptable" and "Needs Improvement" is determined by the department.

Bailey (1985) suggests a system for evaluating faculty performance. See Figure 9.4.

Rating (R)

Assignment Units (AU)						
				3	2	1
Spn	Sum	Fall	Activities	Excellent	Good	Needs Improvement
2	1	1	Teaching		2	
1	2	2	Research	3		
1	1	1	Service		2	
4	4	4				

	AU		R				
Teaching:	4	x	2	=	8	Excellent	31 - 36
Research:	5	x	3	=	15	Good	20 - 30
Service:	3	x	2	=	6	Needs Improvement	0 - 19
			Total		29		

Figure 9.4 - Faculty Performance
Evaluation System

In the plan, each semester (spring, summer, fall) is divided into four, quar-ter-time "assignment units" (AU). To determine a faculty member's score in teaching, research or service*, the total number of AUs accumulated during the year for a given activity is multiplied by the numerical value assigned the rating. For example, as shown in Figure 9.4, the total number of AUs earned for teaching (4) times the assigned value of the rating (2) equals 8. When added to the scores earned for research and service, a total score of 29 results. A score of 29 rates the overall performance of the faculty member for the year as "Good".

The total number of possible points for the faculty evaluation system is the product of the total number of AUs/semester (4) times the number of activities (3) times the highest numerical rating (3). The range of points for "Excellent", "Good" and "Needs Improvement" is determined by the department faculty.

If the salary policies of the institution or college require the grouping or ranking of faculty members in terms of performance, each of the quantitative approaches will assist in the ordering process.

---

* "Professional Practice" will have to be included in the evaluation scheme if the plan is to be adapted to the faculty recognition system.

Tenure and Academic Promotion

Documented success in teaching, research, service and professional practice is essential to being considered for tenure and/or academic promotion. (See Chapter Eight - Promotion Dossier.) Documentation must show sustained effort over an extended period of time in the four areas of activity with an appropriate number of contributions in each area. Whereas salary increases and merit pay are based on an **annual** review of faculty performance, the awarding of tenure and/or promotion is more dependent on the faculty member's record of achievement and balanced **contribution over time.** For the faculty recognition system to function as intended, the annual achievements of the faculty member are compiled for a period of several years with the accumulated results forming the basis for recognition of academic contribution.

As with salary increase and merit pay, the evaluation of performance for purposes of tenure and promotion can be qualitative, quantitative or a combination of both. The faculty member's promotion dossier, curriculum vitae and supporting materials can be reviewed in accordance with qualitative criteria, i.e. sustained effort, balance of contribution, appropriate number of contributions in each area, etc., that result in recommending the awarding of tenure and/or promotion or denying the request.

If a point system is desired, numerical values can be assigned to the criteria and totals or averages computed to assist in the evaluation process. For example, a system could be devised in which a total number of points would have to be accumulated by the faculty member with a minimum number of points earned in each area before tenure and/or promotion could be considered.

Whichever approach is used, it should be agreed upon by a majority of the department faculty and understood by all of them. This is crucial if the potential of the faculty recognition system is to be fully realized.

CHAPTER 10

Suggestions for Implementation

The purpose of this chapter is to reiterate the concepts which are fundamental to the faculty recognition system. To introduce the chapter and put the concepts in context, a review of the purpose and goals of the system seems appropriate.

The two-fold purpose of the faculty recognition system is to assist faculty members in planning, organizing and documenting their professional activities and to establish a basis for recognizing and rewarding faculty accomplishment.

The goals of the system are to:

- Assist faculty members in attaining their professional and career goals;
- Assist academic departments in attaining their organizational goals and continue providing leadership and service to their clientele;
- Foster cooperation in the department by using a system that benefits individual faculty members and the department alike;
- Establish a system for documenting and reporting faculty activities;
- Articulate salary increase, merit pay, tenure and promotion in recognizing faculty accomplishment; and
- Provide a fair and equitable means of evaluating the activities and contributions of faculty members.

Faculty Recognition System

The faculty recognition system is comprised of components which can be used successfully outside of the context of the system. However, when used in concert, the individual components produce an effect that exceeds the total of their separate capabilities. The system provides continuity to the activities of the faculty member. Successful performance that results in annual salary increases and merit pay has a summative value that leads to the granting of tenure and awarding of academic promotion.

In addition, the department benefits. Its organizational goals are realized through the concerted efforts of the faculty. The teaching, research, service and professional practice activities of the faculty member extend the leadership and service functions of the department to its clientele. Students are served. Institutional, professional and community needs are met. The department remains vital.

Integrity

The integrity of the faculty recognition system is the responsibility of the chairperson and faculty members of the department. Whereas the concepts of "system", "articulation" and "continuity" lend an intrinsic value to the organizational approach, the interest and support of all members of the department are essential if the system is to realize its full potential. As a group, the faculty needs to define and agree on the purpose, goals and mission of the department and the needs of the clientele to be served. As individuals, faculty members must pursue activities that support the department, as well as, move them toward their career and professional goals.

The chairperson has the responsibility to provide the necessary leadership to put the faculty recognition system in place. Initially, he/she must guide the faculty in developing the department plan. Following its development, the chairperson then assists the faculty in preparing their annual plans of activity. The annual plans concurrently direct the efforts of the faculty in attaining departmental goals and achieving individual objectives.

In addition, care must be taken by the chairperson during the planning process to establish a basis for more immediate and longer-term recognition of faculty contributions and accomplishments. The annual plan, when realized, should ensure recognition of the teaching, research, service and professional practice activities of the faculty member by way of an increase in salary and receipt of merit pay. Accumulated annual success and a balanced record of productivity in each of the activity areas should result in the eventual receipt of tenure and promotion by the faculty member.

Documentation

If ". . . accumulated annual success and a balanced record of productivity . . ." in teaching, research, service and professional practice are the "doorway" to salary increase, merit pay, tenure and promotion, then documentation of effort is the key. Terms like "accountability," and "verification," come into play when decisions are made regarding a faculty member's contributions. Peer and student evaluations, copies of books, journal articles, research proposals and letters recognizing effort and accomplishment are essential elements in the recognition and reward process.

Care must be taken by faculty members to record their activities as they are accomplished and to file the tangible results for future verification. The documentation effort is not only essential in the formal faculty recognition process, but it also enables individuals to trace their efforts and sense their accomplishments.

Autonomy

The faculty recognition system is a product of the department. Its purpose, goals and mission, as defined in the department plan, establish the parameters within which the corporate department operates and the teaching, research, service and professional practice activities of the faculty occur.

The department plan is not imposed on the faculty by an outside source. Rather, it is a guide developed by the faculty which addresses the needs of its clientele within and outside of the academic community. Within the context of the college and institution, the department is responsible to plan its own direction and to determine its own destiny as it meets the needs of its clientele.

Versatility

Form follows function. If a department considers "Academic Advisement" as department service rather than a part of the teaching function, it should be included under "Department Service". Likewise, professional practice might not be appropriate activity for some departments. If that is the case, the "Professional Practice Activities" section should not be included in their system.

The faculty recognition system is designed to guide the department in planning, organizing and implementing its activities. However, adoption of the system does not limit the department's potential. The purpose and goals of the department must be attained and the objectives of the faculty members realized if the system is to be successful.

Balance

One of the underlying premises of the faculty recognition system is that individual faculty members establish a balanced record of teaching, research, service and professional practice. While a balanced assignment is not necessary each semester, evidence of contribution in each activity over an extended period of time usually precedes an institution's awarding of tenure and/or academic promotion.

"Balance" can be defined in different ways. In some departments, teaching and research are weighted heavier in the evaluation process than service and professional practice. In other departments, the same activities are weighted differently. Regardless, in almost all situations, a faculty member has to have made some contribution in each area of activity before a tenure/promotion recommendation is made.

BIBLIOGRAPHY

1. Appleby, Robert C. (1981). **Modern business administration.** London: Pitman.

2. Bailey, Larry J. (1985). **Faculty performance evaluation system.** Unpublished manuscript. Southern Illinois University, Carbondale.

3. Banathy, Bela H. (1968). **Instructional systems.** Belmont: Fearon.

4. Bortz, Richard F. (1981). **Handbook for developing occupational curricula.** Boston: Allyn and Bacon.

5. Dressel, Paul L. (1976). **Handbook of academic evaluation.** San Francisco: Jossey-Bass.

6. Elman, Sandra E. and Smock, Sue Marx (1985). **Professional service and faculty rewards.** Washington, D.C.: National Association of State Universities and Land-Grant Colleges.

7. Gilmore, Susan K. (1981). Counseling. In Delworth, Ursula; Hansen, Gary R. and Associates, **Student services - a handbook for the profession** (pp. 296-312). San Francisco: Jossey-Bass.

8. Gradussov, Alex (Ed.). (1984). **Personnel management in jamaica.** Unpublished manuscript. College of Arts, Science and Technology, Kingston, Jamaica.

9. Gunn, Bruce (1985). **A participative management evaluation system for appraising faculty performance** (College Student Journal Monograph, Number 1). Chula Vista: Project Innovation.

10. Harris, Robert C. (1977). **Professional survival kit.** Atlantic City: National Association of Industrial Technical Teacher Educators.

11. Jarett, Irwin M., Rader, Daniel W. and Longhurst, Philip, Jr. (1970). **Key factor analysis workbook.** Raleigh: Jarett, Rader and Longhurst.

12. Morrill, Paul Hampton and Spees, Emil R. (1982). **The academic profession.** New York: Human Sciences.

13. Mueller, Kate H. (1961). **Student personnel work in higher education.** Boston: Houghton Mifflin.

14. Nervig, Nordale (1984). **Training, education and development- program structure.** Unpublished manuscript. Southern Illinois University, Carbondale.

15. Partin, Ronald R. (1984). A case study: evaluating faculty at bowling green university. **Change,** Vol. 16/No. 3.

16. Tead, Ordway (1951). **The art of administration.** New York: McGraw-Hill.